# SIX GREEK
# SCULPTORS

PLATE LXVI

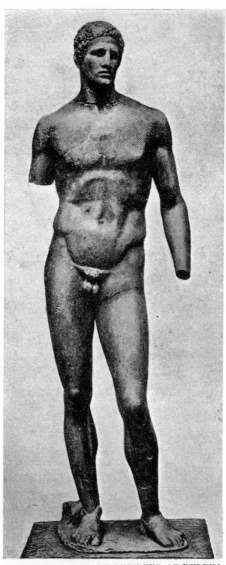

STATUE OF AGIAS, BY LYSIPPUS, AT DELPHI
AFTER *FOUILLES DE DELPHES*, IV., LXIII

*Frontispiece* *See p.* 217

# SIX GREEK SCULPTORS

BY

*1862 – 1939*

ERNEST A. GARDNER, M.A.

YATES PROFESSOR OF ARCHÆOLOGY IN THE UNIVERSITY
OF LONDON ; FORMERLY DIRECTOR OF THE BRITISH SCHOOL
AT ATHENS

*Essay Index Reprint Series*

BOOKS FOR LIBRARIES PRESS, INC.
FREEPORT, NEW YORK

First published 1910
Reprinted 1967

LIBRARY OF CONGRESS CATALOG CARD NUMBER:

67-26744

PRINTED IN THE UNITED STATES OF AMERICA

# PREFACE

To each of the six Greek sculptors from whom this book takes its title a separate volume might well have been assigned in a series such as the present. But when the editor of the series suggested to me that the great. sculptors of Greece should be grouped together, I accepted the suggestion because it seemed that a definite need might thus be met. There are probably many people who wish to acquire some grasp of the character of the chief sculptors, without following the whole course of the history of Greek sculpture from its origins to its decadence ; and there are others who desire to supplement what general outlines of this history they may have learnt by a more vivid realisation and appreciation of the work of the leading artists. There is no need to defend the selection of the six sculptors to whom the chapters of the book are devoted. Alike in their influence on their contem-

poraries and successors, in their place in the estimate
of ancient critics, and in the material we possess for
the study of their work, these six stand out beyond all
rivals, though there are others who excite our imagination and regret, or offer subjects for the most ingenious
and sometimes convincing investigation.

It is impossible to acknowledge my obligation to all
my predecessors, but I would more especially mention
M. Collignon's *Histoire de la Sculpture Grecque*, to
which I have made constant reference, and the various
works of Professor Furtwängler, above all his *Masterpieces of Greek Sculpture*. To Mrs. Strong I am in-
debted for her help in the choice of illustrations, and
for the loan of many photographs; also to both
authors and publisher for permission to reproduce some
details from the magnificent plates of Hamdy-Bey and
Th. Reinach, *Une Nécropole Royale à Sidon*. Other
publications from which I have borrowed are mentioned
in the list of illustrations; I would especially quote
among these the *Fouilles de Delphes*. I must also
acknowledge the permission to photograph and reproduce the statue of Heracles in the Lansdowne collection.
This photograph and also the reproduction of all the

plates have been undertaken by Mr. Emery Walker in a manner which, I trust, speaks for itself. I have to thank my brother, Professor Percy Gardner, for his valuable assistance in revising the proof-sheets.

ERNEST A. GARDNER

UNIVERSITY COLLEGE, LONDON
*December* 1909

# CONTENTS

CHAP.                                           PAGE

I. CHARACTERISTICS OF GREEK SCULPTURE .   .   1

II. EARLY MASTERPIECES .   .   .   .   .   28

III. MYRON .   .   .   .   .   .   .   .   56

IV. PHIDIAS .   .   .   .   .   .   .   79

V. POLYCLITUS .   .   .   .   .   .   117

VI. PRAXITELES .   .   .   .   .   .   140

VII. SCOPAS .   .   .   .   .   .   177

VIII. LYSIPPUS .   .   .   .   .   210

IX. HELLENISTIC SCULPTURE .   .   .   235

INDEX .   .   .   .   .   .   .   253

# ILLUSTRATIONS

**PLATE**                                      **PAGE**

66. Statue of Agias, by Lysippus, at Delphi. After *Fouilles de Delphes*, IV., LXIII. *Frontispiece*

1. Head of Vatican Meleager (Græco-Roman copy); Head of Villa Medici Meleager (Greek Version). After *Antike Denkmäler*, I., Pl. XL.   .    .    .    .    *To face*   5

2. Bronze statuette in the British Museum : Apollo with the Stag .    .    .    .    ,,  19

3. Bronze statuette in the British Museum .    ,,  20

4. Female figure from the Acropolis at Athens   .    .    .    .    .    .    ,,  21

5. Frieze of the "Treasury of the Cnidians" at Delphi ; Battle of Gods and Giants. After *Fouilles de Delphes*, IV., XIII.   .    ,,  29

6. Metope of the Treasury of the Athenians at Delphi ; Heracles and the Cerynian Stag. After *Fouilles de Delphes*, IV., XLI. .    .    .    .    .    .    ,,  33

7. Head of warrior, probably Æginetan, from the Acropolis at Athens   .    .    .    ,,  47

8. Bronze Charioteer at Delphi .    .    .    ,,  49

PLATE                                                              PAGE

9. Head of Bronze Charioteer at Delphi    .    *To face*  50

10. Relief from the "Ludovisi Throne"      .      „      53

11. Discobolus, after Myron ; bronze cast from
       statue in the Vatican; head from
       Massimi statue  .    .    .    .    .      „      61

12. Discobolus, after Myron ; restored cast ;
       Torso from statue in Museo delle
       Terme ; head from Massimi statue    .    „      63

13. Head of Massimi Discobolus  .    .    .    „      64

14. Marsyas, after Myron ; bronze statuette in
       the British Museum  .    .    .    .      „      67

15. Marble statuette of Hercules  .    .    .    „      73

16. Metope of the Parthenon: Lapith and
       Centaur  .    .    .    .    .    .      „      75

17. Diomed with the Palladium ; statue in
       Munich  .    .    .    .    .    .      „      77

18. "Riccardi Head." Style of Myron    .      „      78

19. "Strangford Shield," in British Museum      „      82

20. Head of Athena, in Jacobsen Collection,
       Copenhagen  .    .    .    .    .      „      87

21. Small copy of Athena Parthenos in
       Madrid  .    .    .    .    .    .      „      90

22. Iris, Demeter, and Persephone, from the
       E. Pediment of the Parthenon  .    .      „      98

23. Figure from W. Pediment of Parthenon .      „      100

24. Chariot horses from S. Frieze of Parthenon    „      103

PLATE                         PAGE

25. Athenian Knights, from W. Frieze of
Parthenon . . . . . . *To face* 104

26. Youths with Cows, from N. Frieze of
Parthenon . . . . . . „ 105

27. Head of Zeus, in Boston . . . . „ 108

28. "Lemnian Athena"; statue in Dresden,
with Bologna head added . . . „ 111

29. "Lemnian Athena"; head in Bologna . „ 112

30. Apollo, in the Museo delle Terme at
Rome . . . . . . . „ 114

31. Head of Apollo, in the Museo delle
Terme at Rome . . . . . „ 115

32. Side of "Lycian Sarcophagus," from
Sidon in Constantinople. After Hamdy-
Bey and Reinach, *Nécropole Royal à
Sidon*, Pl. XVI. . . . . . .. 116

33. Heads from "Lycian Sarcophagus."
After Hamdy-Bey and Reinach, *op.
cit.*, detail on Pl. XIV. . *Between pp.* 116 *and* 117

34. Doryphorus, after Polyclitus, at Naples . *To face* 122

35. Diadumenus. After Polyclitus, from
Delos . . . . . . . „ 124

36. Head of Diadumenus, in Dresden . . „ 125

37. Head of Diadumenus, in British Museum „ 127

38. "Westmacott Athlete," in British Museum „ 129

39. Head of Athlete ("Nelson Head") . „ 130

PLATE                                                          PAGE

40. Bronze Head from Beneventum, in the
    Louvre   .    .    .    .  *Between pp.* 130 *and* 131

41. Amazon after Polyclitus in Lansdowne
    House   .   .   .   .   .   *To face* 131

42. Head of Amazon, in Lansdowne House  .   ,,   132

43. Hermes, by Praxiteles, at Olympia .  .   ,,   143

44. Head of Hermes, by Praxiteles  .  .   ,,   146

45. Aphrodite of Cnidus. After Praxiteles, in
    Vatican (from a cast) .   .   .   .   ,,   152

46. Head of Aphrodite, "Kaufmann Head."
    After *Antike Denkmäler*, I., XLI.   .   ,,   157

47. Head of Aphrodite (or Phryne), "Pet-
    worth Head"  .   .   .   .   ,,   158

48. Torso of Aphrodite, type of Venus of
    Arles, in Athens  .   .   .   .   ,,   159

49. Side of "Sarcophagus of Mourning
    Women," from Sidon.   After Hamdy-
    Bey and Reinach, *Nécropole Royale à
    Sidon*, Pl. VII. .   .   .   .   ,,   173

50. Portrait of a lady, from Herculaneum, in
    Dresden  .   .   .   .   .   ,,   174

51. Head of Heracles, from Tegea, by Scopas.
    After *Bulletin de Corr. Hellénique*,
    1901, VII. .   .   .   .   .   ,,   183

52. Mænad, after Scopas. After *Mélanges
    Perrot*, Pl. V.  .   .   .   .   ,,   188

53. Head of Demeter of Cnidus, in British
    Museum  .   .   .   .   .   .   ,,   192

PLATE                            PAGE

54. " Ares Ludovisi " . . . *Between pp.* 196 *and* 197

55. Head of " Ares Ludovisi " . . . *To face* 197

56. Heracles, in Lansdowne House . . ,, 198

57. Head of Lansdowne Heracles . *Between pp.* 198 *and* 199

58. Head of Lansdowne Heracles . . . *To face* 199

59. Head, probably of Artemisia, from Mausoleum . . . . ,, 204

60. Charioteer, from Frieze of Mausoleum . ,, 205

61. Frieze of Mausoleum ; Battle of Greeks and Amazons . . . . . ,, 206

62. Frieze of Mausoleum; Battle of Greeks and Amazons . . . *Between pp.* 206 *and* 207

63. Frieze of Mausoleum; Battle of Greeks and Amazons . . . *Between pp.* 206 *and* 207

64. Apollo, from Mausoleum . . . *To face* 207

65. Stele from the Ilissus at Athens . . ,, 208

67. Head of Agias. After *Fouilles de Delphes,* IV., LXIV. . . . . . ,, 218

68. " Apoxyomenos," in Vatican . . . ,, 220

69. Head of Alexander, in British Museum . ,, 225

70. Alexander in combat, from Sidon Sarcophagus. Detail from Hamdy-Bey and Reinach, *Nécropole Royale à Sidon,* Pl. XXX. . . . . . ,, 227

PLATE                                                        PAGE

71. Head of Alexander; Detail from Hamdy-
    Bey and Reinach, *op. cit.*, Pl. XXXIII.

                          *Between pp.* 228 *and* 229

72. Head of Persian; Detail from Hamdy-Bey
    and Reinach, *op. cit.*, Pl. XXXII.    .   *To face* 229

73. Statue of a Youth, from Subiaco   .   .    "   238

74. Disc with Death of Niobids, in British
    Museum   .    .    .    .    .    .   "   241

75. A Son of Niobe, in Florence  .   .   .   "   242

76. Head, in British Museum    .   .   .   "   243

77. Head of bronze Hermes, at Naples   .  "   244

78. Bronze statue, from wreck off Cerigotto,
    in Athens  .    .    .    .    .    .   "   245

79. Victory, from Samothrace, in the Louvre   "   246

80. Dying Gaul, in Capitoline Museum, Rome   "   248

81. Head of Warrior, in British Museum   .  "   250

# CHAPTER I

## CHARACTERISTICS OF GREEK SCULPTURE

In any history, and above all in the history of art, there are two main aspects from which the subject may be considered. We may either devote ourselves to the study of general tendencies, the development of types and ideas, their national character, and the circumstances that surrounded and fostered their growth; or we may concentrate our attention on the attainments of individuals, realise as far as possible their aims and their personality, and the contributions which they respectively made to the general progress. It is true that in any comprehensive study the two must be blended, must supplement and confirm each other; and that whichever principle we may adopt to guide the selection and arrangement of the facts, we cannot follow it to the entire exclusion of the other. In artistic production it may seem at first sight that the genius of the individual master is less trammelled and circumscribed than that of a political or social reformer. Yet the artist is no less dependent upon external circumstances for the occasion and the material of his works. But for the defeat of the Persian invasion there would not have been that exaltation of national sentiment which finds its symbolical expression in the sculptures of the Parthenon ; but for the Persian spoils and the accumulated treasures of the Delian league, there would have been no resources available for the execution of the colossal statues of Phidias. And this material side is not the most important. Had not their predecessors worked through generations of experiment and observation to improve the familiar types, to attain mastery over the stubborn substance of marble and bronze, and to acquire and perfect a skilled technique in the treatment of the nude and of drapery, no sculptor of the fifth century could have conceived or executed the bold yet symmetrical contortions of the *Discobolus*, or the exquisite grace of the *Fates* in the Parthenon pediment. To us these things are the beginning of all that is best in art, and vindicate for Myron and for Phidias their acknowledged position as the earliest among the great masters of sculpture. But they are also the end of a long and laborious development. Had Myron and Phidias been born a century earlier, they could no more have produced these works than if they had lived at the present day.

But, such considerations apart, the study of the great masters themselves is profitable as well as fascinating. In the earlier days of our modern appreciation of Greek art, in the latter part of the eighteenth and the beginning of the nineteenth centuries, there was not much historical discrimination of styles and periods; it is significant that one of the earliest books which brought order into the chaos, and on which all subsequent study is based, was a history of artists, Brunn's "Geschichte der griechischen Künstler." This was, no doubt, partly owing to the fact that only in this way was it possible to collect and order systematically all the scattered references to the history of art in classical literature, and so to construct a chronological framework into which a study of the extant monuments could be fitted. Since then we have had many histories of art, in which the great sculptors have, of course, been considered each in his place; in the present volume, on the other hand, they will be considered one at a time, with a view rather to realising their personal attainments and artistic character, so far as it can be ascertained from their extant works, or copies of them, and from the testimony of their contemporaries and successors. In this way it may also be possible to appreciate more clearly their place in the general course of development, and their contribution to the characteristic excellence of Greek sculpture.

Before we approach the study of individual masters it may be advisable to take a more general survey of the character of Greek sculpture, as contrasted with earlier and later styles. This is the more necessary because of certain prejudices that exist, and that have been endorsed, in whole or in part, by some of the greatest art teachers of our time. Chief among these is a false conception of " the antique," as it is commonly presented to students in art schools, too frequently without any teaching to make its study intelligent and educative. Sometimes casts of Greek sculpture are used as a mere exercise in drawing, and the intellectual and æsthetic training is subordinated to the purely mechanical; frequently, too—though not, I believe, at the present day among those who have any practical acquaintance with the matter—the prejudice against them is increased by the supposition that they are held up for imitation to the exclusion of the student's own observation of nature. Moreover, the casts so selected are not infrequently from works of inferior merit—often indeed from works restored so as to have no claim to be called " antique " at all. They are, indeed, mostly taken from well-known statues; but how remote such statues may be from the originals that they represent may be realised by a most instruc-tive comparison in the case of one of them, the

PLATE I

HEAD OF VATICAN MELEAGER
GRÆCO-ROMAN COPY

HEAD OF VILLA MEDICI MELEAGER
GREEK VERSION

AFTER *ANTIKE DENKMAELER*, I. PL. XL

*To face p.* 5

*Meleager* of the Vatican. Other copies exist of the head of this statue; and one of them, now placed on a statue to which it does not belong in the Villa Medici at Rome, is, if not the original, at least so near to it in the date of its execution and in the spirit of its expression as to enable us to realise what the original was like. We have only to place these two examples of the same head side by side to see what is the relation of a Græco-Roman copy to a Greek statue. The Vatican *Meleager* shows just the perfection of form, the absence of individuality, the vacancy of expression and character, the vapid generalisation of type, which modern critics are too often wont to regard as the usual qualities of " the antique." But we have only to look at the Medici head to see that these qualities do not belong to the original, but have been imported into it by the copyist, who evidently had a conception of the Greek art he was copying, not unlike that of many modern critics and of some modern imitators of classical art. In the Medici head we see the very opposite of all these qualities; the forms show less perfection, more individuality, and, above all, the expression is full of character, and shows a passionate and fiery nature, realised and reproduced with a marvellous directness of observation. Both are, in a sense, ideal works; but the one is the fresh and vigorous embodiment of the master's conception of this passionate head; the other is the cold and academic generalisation of a conventional school. In many cases we have only later copies like this Vatican *Meleager* to guide us; and it is necessary to realise how much allowance we must make before quoting them as evidence for the work of the Greek masters themselves.

From these and other causes there is, no doubt, a general feeling, even among educated people who have made no study of the subject, that Greek sculpture deals with cold and colourless generalisation, that, to quote Ruskin, "there is no personal character in true Greek art—abstract ideas of youth and age, strength and swiftness, virtue and vice—yes; but there is no individuality." The best answer to this charge is a careful study of Greek art; but its origin, apart from the influences already mentioned, is, I think, to be found in an expressed or implied contrast with Tuscan or with modern sculpture; with the art which sought

> To bring the invisible full into play,
> Let the visible go to the dogs—what matters?

or the art which regards any departure from the individual model as a sin against artistic truth. This is a matter to which we must return later; for the present we are rather concerned with the characteristic excellence of Greek sculpture than with its alleged defects or its contrast with mediæval or modern work. This excellence is universally admitted in the case of fifth-century work, and especially of the Elgin marbles, which have compelled the admiration of critics of every school and of sculptors as far removed from one another as Canova and Rodin. But there is a tendency, especially at the present day, to withhold due appreciation not only from the ordinary run of Hellenistic and Græco-Roman work, but even from Praxiteles himself. To a Greek such a preference would have seemed an absurdity; he would not have dreamt of comparing mere architectural sculptures, such as those of the Parthenon, with the masterpieces of the fourth century; if he were asked to name the most representative sculptors of Greece, he would very likely have named Polyclitus, Praxiteles, Scopas, and Lysippus even before Phidias himself when his colossal statues were still extant. It may be that time and chance have in this instance led us to a truer judgment. But if we would appreciate Greek sculpture as a whole, we must not regard it as beginning and ending with some thirty years in the middle of the fifth century.

It may be instructive in this context to remember that the men to whom we owe the first impulse to a scientific and systematic appreciation of Greek art— Winckelmann and Lessing and their contemporaries

—knew nothing of the Elgin marbles ; to them Greek
sculpture was represented by the *Apollo Belvedere*,[1]
the *Venus de' Medici*, or the *Laocoon.* Yet from works
like these, which to us sometimes seem more fitted to
be quoted as warnings against the defects of Greek art
in its decline, they drew just and far-reaching inferences
as to the character of its excellence ; and these inferences have been confirmed rather than set aside by a
fuller knowledge of the work of the best period.  The
same qualities which we admire in the sculptures of the
Parthenon must be present, though in a less degree, in
Hellenistic and Græco-Roman works ; and we cannot
but respect the insight and receptiveness which caught,
even from things like these, the spirit that inspired
Greek sculpture as a whole.   But the detailed criticism
of a century or more ago often falls short of its power
of appreciation, and is responsible for some of the
prejudices and misconceptions of the present day—
especially in its too indiscriminate praise of an academic
generalisation of forms which loses touch with the
realities of nature ; we may take as an example
Winckelman's suggestion that the absence of veins in
Greek statues of the gods was intended to imply a

    The *Apollo Belvedere* is by many regarded as a copy of a fourth-
century original.   But even if this view be correct, the extant statue
and Winckelmann's appreciation of its character may be quoted in
this connection.

glorified or transfigured body—a suggestion that collapses of itself now that we know this peculiarity to be absent from statues of the gods of the best period and to be merely characteristic of a certain phase of Hellenistic art.

This view of academic generalisation, whether rightly or wrongly regarded as characteristic of Greek art, is directly at variance with both the theory and the practice of many modern artists and critics, who hardly regard any departure from the model as justifiable, who say, for example, that "it is a mistake to try to improve on nature"; a saying doubtless true in a sense, but capable of a very narrow and misleading application, and one which, if applied too literally, reduces the artist to a mere machine. Here, as in other similar cases, it is probable that the truth lies between the two extremes. But at present it is not so much our aim to investigate the true theory and correct practice of the art of sculpture as to ascertain, as far as possible, what were the main principles that guided the Greek sculptors and led to their unrivalled excellence.

Apart from the imagination and invention of the artist and his technical skill in dealing with the material in which his work is to be executed, we may say that there are three main factors that contribute to the creation of a work of art—convention, observation, and selection. The character of each of these three, their combination with one another, and the degree to which they affect the artist, are to a great extent due to circumstances over which he has little or no control. The conditions that lead to the happiest results seem to consist of a due harmony in the contributions of all three elements; and I believe that the characteristic excellence of Greek Sculpture is due to such harmony. It is easy enough to see how an absence of such harmony, an undue preponderance of one or other of the influences, may tend to the detriment of art. Perhaps the most obvious and familiar example is that of Egypt, where, after the early dynasties, the art of sculpture was reduced to a mechanical canon, and the same types were reproduced again and again in lifeless monotony. There was, indeed, variety in size and in technical skill of execution; but, so far at least as monumental sculpture is concerned, no direct contact with nature, no room for the individual observation of the artist. But much Græco-Roman art, and through imitation of it modern classical art of the conventional type, is really in much the same case. The defect here is not at first sight so obvious, because the originals from which the imitations are derived are less mannered and nearer in touch with nature, so that the artificial character of the imitations may easily be overlooked

and their truth to their originals mistaken for truth to
nature. It is this misconception that we have already
noticed as in a great degree responsible for the reaction
on the part of some modern artists and critics towards
the view that all Greek art is conventional and lacking
in individuality. The detriment to art of a too strict
adherence to convention is generally admitted; but the
danger, on the other hand, of a too great freedom from
convention, of too exclusive dependence on individual
observation, is not so universally recognised, and is by
some emphatically denied. I venture to think, however, that it is just as real as the other, and that it is
the cause of the chaos which we see in a modern exhi-
bition of sculpture. This absence of fixed types and
recognised conventions is one of the reasons why the
modern public is so bewildered in its study of modern
sculpture, and finds just appreciation so hard to attain,
and why a modern sculptor finds it so difficult to produce work that is both dignified and original. In the
greatest age of sculpture in Greece, as in the greatest
age of painting at the Italian Renaissance, the most
original artists were often content to reproduce again
and again, with slight variation, a limited number of
well-known types.

Bacon says that " men's thoughts are made according
to their inclination; their discourse and speeches

according to their learning and infused opinions; but their deeds are often as they have been accustomed." If we apply this saying to art, I think we may assert that men draw or model as they have been taught, and observe as they have been accustomed; what they do as they please is in this case frequently eliminated. Doubtless imagination is free; but the form it takes and the means by which it is expressed depend greatly on external conditions. That neither observation nor technique is untrammelled by circumstances is evident; one has only to think of the way the same subject would be rendered by a Greek, a Japanese, and a modern impressionist. Each may faithfully render what he sees; but what he sees is different in each case. And this difference will be found not only in the works of trained artists, but also in the first attempts of children or the crude productions of " the man in the street." *Graffiti* on walls are often just as characteristic of national or local style as finished pictures. Even observation, then, is not a matter that depends entirely on the individual artist; he must be affected by the custom of his compatriots and his contemporaries, as well as by the perception and tastes which he inherits from his predecessors. It is virtually impossible for a man to depend on his own observation alone; if he attempts to do so, he often places himself

at the mercy of fortuitous and often disadvantageous
surroundings, instead of having to guide him a tradition
which, if it sometimes confines him too narrowly, saves
him from losing his way altogether. The relations
of tradition and observation have been put in a new
light by Professor Löwy's suggestive book on "The
Representation of Nature in Early Greek Art." He
points out that neither the child nor the primitive
draughtsman represents, as a rule, what he sees before
him. They produce rather what may be called a
memory picture, which contains the most familiar or the
most essential features of the object represented. It
is owing to this principle, for example, that it is so
common in early art to find the body of a man represented from the front, while his legs are in profile. It
is impossible to discuss here Professor Löwy's statement and illustration of this theory; it is for the most
part both convincing and illuminating. But its application to the history and development of sculpture is
a more complicated and in some ways a more disputable
matter. There is no doubt, for example, that the rigid
position and square shape of many early statues is
due to the fact that they embody the two main aspects
of the figure, the front view and the profile. And this
limitation persists to some extent throughout the
best period of Greek sculpture; it is not until the

Hellenistic age that we find statues and groups that are really thought out and composed in the round.   In the case of sculpture in relief the limitations or conventions are still more persistent.   An early relief is often a mere silhouette, with the ground cut away round its outlines ; and in this way there comes into being the conventional front plane which was the original surface of the slab, and which is the controlling condition of all the finest Greek reliefs ; for example, of the Parthenon frieze.   Depth of effect, the giving of an atmosphere within the relief, is precluded by this limitation ; and we do not really find it broken through until the Flavian age of Roman sculpture ; for example, in the reliefs of the Arch of Titus.   Are we in such a case to recognise continuous advance in the freedom and the resources of the art of sculpture ?   Or should we rather maintain that the earlier sculptors, consciously or unconsciously, adhered to these conventions as the canons and principles of their art, and that the violation of these canons is not to be regarded as an advance, but as a loss of the finer instinct for what is fitting, and therefore most satisfying to the eye and to the intelligence ?   Neither opinion is tenable in its extreme form.   The theory of continuous advance seems to imply as its underlying assumption that impressionism or illusionism is the ultimate aim of art.

Even if this be granted, the matter is not so simple as it seems. The primitive artist, in reproducing his memory-picture, seeks to produce on his public the same impression that has been produced in his own mind; and this surely is impressionism according to one of its definitions. Again, Lysippus is said to have made an advance on his predecessors by representing men as they appear to the eye, not as they actually are—"ab illis factos quales essent homines, a se quales viderentur esse"; and this is another essential principle of impressionism. In both these cases the artist avoids representing an object exactly as it is in nature; but in the one instance unconsciously, because he has not yet attained to full powers of observation and expression; in the other instance consciously, because he regards this as the best way of attaining his artistic aim. And what applies to the two artists applies also to the different publics for which they are respectively working. It has been said that the power of selection—a confident and accurate knowledge what to express, even more than how to express it—distinguishes the master from the student in art. And this power of selection undoubtedly contributes to illusion in a very high degree. But here also convention and custom play their part; and a work of art, whether painting or sculpture, or of any other kind, will miss its aim if it is

too far removed from what is looked for by the artist's
contemporaries or compatriots.    At its highest, art
does indeed rise beyond all conventions and limitations
and creates something that is "not for an age, but for
all time." Yet even this highest creation can be better
understood if we realise the conditions under which it
came to be made.

The character of Greek art, as has already been said,
is to a great extent derived from its happy combination
of tradition and observation.    In order to realise this
fact, it seems advisable to consider more in detail the
circumstances that led to this combination, and the
historical and social conditions under which tradition
was transmitted, and favourable opportunities were
given for observation.    Even before anything which
we can call Greek sculpture had begun to exist, it was
customary to fill every local shrine with innumerable
votive offerings, and many of them were in human or
animal form.    The meaning of these we need not now
discuss; many of them were probably intended to
represent deities; and, in addition to them, there was
usually in the temple an image of the deity to whom it
was dedicated.    This may have been in the earliest
times an aniconic symbol or fetish; but it very soon came
to have some resemblance to human form; for the
tendency of the Greeks was always towards anthropo-

morphism, whether in religion or imagination. As soon
as the skill of the sculptor was far enough advanced,
there was thus an abundance of demand for his productions, with the additional advantage that their form
was already prescribed by ritual or custom within
certain limits. This was particularly the case with the
temple statues; but it was not these, at least at first,
that offered scope for the development of sculpture.
It was rather the multitude of votive statues or
statuettes, and among these, in Greece as in Cyprus,
Rhodes and elsewhere, there were probably skilled
examples of foreign workmanship among the rude
attempts of native artificers. Whether by these or
other means, it is certain that the primitive Greek
sculptor, at home as well as in the eastern and southern
colonies, came to be acquainted with the types and
conventions of earlier art, especially of the art of
Egypt. The immediate effect upon his work may
be seen by comparing such a statuette of primitive
Greek workmanship with its Egyptian prototype; we
find almost every detail imitated; the only difference
lies in the skill of the artisan. The borrowing of
Egyptian methods is attested, in the case of the family
of Rhœcus of Samos, by the story that his two sons,
Telecles and Theodorus, made the two halves of a
statue separately, one of them being at the time in

B

Samos, the other at Ephesus, and that the two parts, when put together, harmonised so as to appear the work of a single man. This story, if true, certainly seems to imply an adoption of the artificial Egyptian canon of proportions for the figure: and Rhœcus, the father, may well have studied this canon during a visit to Egypt, where his native place, Samos, had a share in the colony of Naucratis.[1] The early Greek sculptors borrowed not only the proportions and some points of technique, but also a limited number of types, which they repeated again and again with variety of meaning. If we wish to see how lifeless and mechanical such borrowed types can be, we only have to look at any collection of Cypriote statues. But the Greek sculptor, even from the first, never copied in this mechanical manner. It is true that, owing to the small number of selected types, and their frequent repetition, there seems, at first sight, a certain monotony about the attempts of archaic Greek sculpture. There is, however, a vital distinction between them and mere mechanical repetitions such as we see in Cyprus; this is the promise of advance and improvement that is found in the one and not in the other. If we try to

---

1 As a confirmation of this may be quoted the fact that, when excavating in the Temple of Aphrodite at Naucratis, I found a bowl dedicated by Rhœcus.

PLATE II

*To face p.* 19

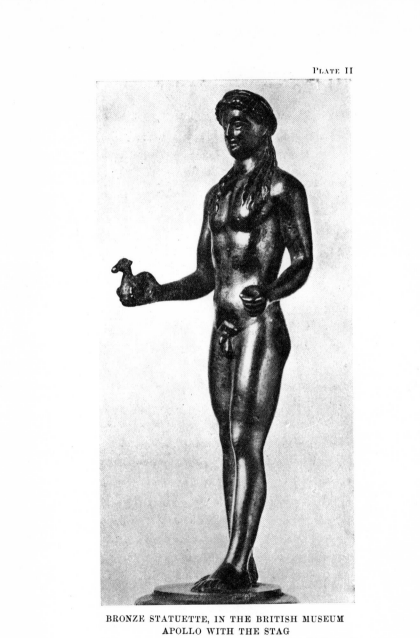

BRONZE STATUETTE, IN THE BRITISH MUSEUM
APOLLO WITH THE STAG

analyse more closely wherein exactly this promise lies,
we shall find that almost every archaic statue in Greece
bears a trace in some part or other of direct study and
observation of nature; it may be in the treatment of
hands or knee-joints or toes, or in the fold of skin at
the elbow; but it is rarely, if ever, absent; and it shows
that the artist, while content to repeat the conventional
type, tried to make it his own, to give it some individual
stamp, by adding to it something, however insignificant,
of his own direct observation. Thus, by not diffusing
his skill over an effort beyond his power, but con-
centrating it on a restricted field, well within his
compass, he made a real contribution to the general
advance in the knowledge of anatomy, and in the
struggle with the material, whether wood or stone or
marble, clay or bronze. And, owing to the grouping
of artists in families and schools, to the prominent
place of sculpture in the life of the nation, and the constant opportunities afforded by the various shrines, which
served as perpetual exhibitions of art, each advance,
when once gained, was not easily lost again, and the
whole mass of Greek sculpture moved steadily onwards,
towards that mastery, both in knowledge and technique
which was necessary before the great sculptors of the
fifth century could fulfil their destiny.

As the skill of the artist increased, he became more

venturesome; he tried to realise for himself, and to improve in rendering, the proportions of limbs and body, the position of bones and muscles in the torso.  At first he did this only in the rigidly erect position, with no variety except that which was in the foreign type which he borrowed, with its left foot advanced ; but even so, the hips were on the same level.  Then, by degrees, the variety offered by this pose was grasped ; one hip was allowed to be slightly higher than the other, as the weight was divided unevenly between the two legs ; and, this change once introduced, the central line of the body could no longer remain rigidly vertical, but acquired the elastic curve which we find already in works of the transitional age, and which is merely further developed in the statues of Polyclitus and even of Praxiteles.  A single type has served us so far for illustration, but it was the type which is the most characteristic of early Greek sculpture, and which offered most opportunity for its development—a type too of almost universal application, as it served alike for god or for athlete, for dedication in a shrine, or for a monument over a tomb.  It would be possible to trace a similar evolution in the case of the draped figure and its drapery, noticing how the forms of the figure were gradually realised through the drapery that at first envelops them like a solid mass ; how the various tex-

PLATE III

BRONZE STATUETTE, IN THE BRITISH MUSEUM

*To face p. 20*

PLATE IV

FEMALE FIGURE, FROM THE ACROPOLIS
AT ATHENS

*To face p.* 21

ture of wool and linen, of finer and thicker stuff, was rendered first by mere conventional parallel lines, closer together or farther apart, and then gradually varied and made more natural, until it reached first the refined delicacy of Attic work of the early fifth century, and then the mastery which we see in the pediments of the Parthenon. But one type suffices to illustrate the general character of the development. It was not, however, only by thus fostering the concentration of effort that conservatism of types contributed to the advance of art. It also had a most important influence on the technique of sculpture, especially in marble. For the very fixity of the type led to a freedom of hand in the execution, such as could be attained in no other way. When a sculptor, trained in the production of these types, set to work upon a new statue, he did not need to make a wax or clay model, or to transfer its shape to his block of stone by any mechanical appliances or calculations. He was so familiar with his subject that he could go straight at his block of marble free-hand ; it was not until it was to a great extent roughed out that individual niceties of finish came into play ; and when he did come to these, it was with the facility and confidence inspired by the ready performance of a familiar task. And, even if he did spoil a block, as must sometimes have been the case, the loss was not so great as in

a costly imported material.   Marble of various qualities
is found in many different parts of Greece, and almost
all were used at first by the local artists, though in later
times the superiority of a few quarries, such as those
of Paros and Pentelicus, caused them to be usually
employed for sculpture.

Nor do these conditions apply only to the archaic
period; we find equally free-hand work in unfinished
statues of a later period also.   And the reason is partly
the same.   Even in later times, though the artists were
much more free to give scope to their individual bent,
there was a constant demand for slight variations upon
well-known types, very often based upon original works
by the great masters.   Such statues, neither exact copies
nor truly original works, are familiar to us from the
ordinary contents of our museums.   And a sculptor,
asked to produce such a statue, would be able, if
familiar with the ordinary répertoire of sculpture
and trained in one of the great local schools, to
go straight to work upon his marble block without
hesitation.   All this applies, of course, only in a
limited degree to the original creations of the great
masters.   But they too had gone through the same
training, and acquired their confidence and facility
by the same methods of work; paradoxical as it
may seem at first sight, the very freedom of Greek

sculpture is to a great extent due to its close adherence to tradition.

It is, of course, none the less true that tradition alone is lifeless. No art, and especially that of sculpture, can make true progress unless it be constantly kept in touch with nature by observation. Here again the social surroundings of the Greek artist gave him an immense advantage over all others. The daily exercises in the palæstra or gymnasium and the frequently recurring athletic festivals gave him constant opportunities for observing the human form both in rest and action, and this too in perfection of condition and of all-round muscular development; and with the help of a well-trained memory he gained a variety in truth to nature such as no study of a posed model can ever give, that very *multiplicata veritas* which is noted by critics as one of the chief attainments of Myron. For the observation of drapery, too, he had constant opportunities in the figures that surrounded him in daily life; and there he could see a variety and grace of texture and of folds such as no draping of a model in unfamiliar garments and materials could ever have suggested. It is true that the same opportunities for varied observation did not exist in the case of the nude female figure; and it is perhaps for this very reason that Greek statues of this type, however beautiful in

form, rarely if ever impress us with the same breadth
and nobility of conception as the corresponding male
figures, whether of gods or men. The feeling of the
Greeks themselves about the matter is well illustrated
by the story of Zeuxis at Croton, how the people of that
town, when they commissioned him to paint a picture of
Helen, and wished to give him every opportunity for
excelling himself in such a subject, allowed him to see a
selection of the most beautiful of their maidens just as
freely as he could see their brothers exercising in the
palæstra. This is evidently the meaning of the story,
though it is misinterpreted by some later authorities in
accordance with the eclectic spirit of their own age.

This brings us to the question of selection—a question
which requires careful consideration, because misunder-
standings may easily occur about it.   Lucian, usually
a good art critic, makes a lapse about this matter
that may serve as a warning; in describing a wuman
of ideal beauty, he selects for her various features
and characteristics from various famous statues—the
form of head and face generally from the *Cnidian
Aphrodite* of Praxiteles, the cheeks and hands from
the *Aphrodite in the Gardens* of Alcamenes, the outline
of the face and proportion of the nose from the *Lemnia*
of Phidias, the mouth and neck from the same sculptor's
*Amazon,* the nameless grace of the smile and expression

of modesty from the *Sosandra* of Calamis, and so on.
He realises, however, himself that a figure so composed
would be not a work of art but a monstrosity. The
author of the *Ad Herennium* was nearer the mark when
he said, "Chares did not learn the art of sculpture from
Lysippus by his master showing him a head by Myron,
an arm by Praxiteles, a chest by Polyclitus, and so
on, but he saw his master at work on all kinds of things,
and, of himself, he could study the works of others."
The eclecticism implied in such suggestion, whether
accepted or rejected, is actually to be seen in some
Hellenistic or Græco-Roman statues, but the incongruity
of the various parts is often obvious. When, however,
the selection is made, not from earlier works of art
but from various living models, it may seem at first
sight more subtle and more defensible; but it is really
contrary both to nature and to art. This kind of
selection, as understood by the later eclectics, must
then be altogether excluded from consideration. But
selection, in its proper use, is an essential part of all
artistic production. Even a modern artist who follows
his model exactly in every detail must at least allow
himself to select a suitable model. This is the case
even with a photograph, a cast from life, or any other
mechanical reproduction. It does not, however, seem
to have been a method ever adopted by the Greeks,

even as an aid to sculptors, at least until the Hellenistic
age, and then, too, to a very limited degree.  A Greek
sculptor so familiarised himself with living and moving
forms, so stored his memory with the outline and
surface modelling of every part he might require, that
he was able, his theme or subject once selected and
composed, to cut straight to it in the marble, just as
Michael Angelo also is said to have done.  He was
thus able not to copy nature but to create after nature,
and hence he attained freedom in his work and a
harmony between its various parts.  Whether he
actually worked with a model before him or not is a
matter on which it is impossible to obtain any trustworthy information; but, if he did, it was only to
correct or supplement some observation in detail.
Yet his work was not an academic generalisation; it
was always, in the best times, dependent upon the
artist's own observation, though both his eye and his
hand had doubtless been trained by familiarity with the
work of his predecessors.  And he was thus enabled to
create figures which, though the perfection of their
proportions was perhaps beyond what could be found
in any individual, yet had a life and individuality of
their own, based upon the master's familiarity with his
subject and his exact realisation of its character.  The
modern advocates of close adherence to the model in

sculpture are unwilling to admit that any good work
can be done from memory and selection. An appeal to
the analogy of another art may perhaps be allowed
here. No one maintains that it is impossible for a
dramatist or a novelist to create a real and life-like
character without reproducing in detail the character
and even the physical type of some person whom he
studies and who serves as his model. May not a statue
made in this way have as much individuality as a character in a play or a novel, though in this latter case an
actual model is not usually thought desirable or necessary? A similar freedom in artistic creation is, of course,
only possible to the sculptor who has as free and plenti-
ful opportunities for observing the living form as the
dramatist or novelist has of studying manners and
character. But this advantage is just what the sculptor
in Greece possessed to a degree that has never been
attainable by any of his successors of a later age.

# CHAPTER II

## EARLY MASTERPIECES

In the last chapter we have seen something of the conditions under which the art of sculpture arose in Greece, and of the influences that were to lead to its unrivalled perfection. The growth was indeed a very rapid one; but the masterpieces of the sculptors of the fifth century, viewed by themselves, often show little trace of the process through which the art that created them had itself been evolved. The pedimental figures from the Parthenon, for example, seem to show a perfection in human form and in drapery such as does not readily suggest development leading up to it; they transcend all local and temporal conditions, and therefore it seems almost superfluous, at first sight, to think of their history or surroundings. Yet even among the Elgin marbles there are some reminders of human imperfection, and therefore of the possibility of rise and decline; some of the metopes, for example, show distinct survivals of the awkwardness or stiffness of archaic schools, though they

PLATE V

FRIEZE OF THE "TREASURY OF THE CNIDIANS" AT DELPHI; BATTLE OF GODS AND
GIANTS.  AFTER *FOUILLES DE DELPHES*, IV., XIII

*To face p.* 29.

show also the promise that was to be fufilled in other
parts of the same building. We shall therefore be more
in a position to understand and to appreciate the work of
the great sculptors of the fifth century B.c. if we first
take a brief survey of a few of the works that were being
made in Greece just before their time, or while they were
still serving their apprenticeship to their art.

Many of these early works are architectural sculptures,
as, indeed, are the Elgin marbles themselves. But
some of them were almost certainly designed by well-
known sculptors, though the execution must in many
cases have been left to assistants, and we can sometimes
recognise this fact in the inequality or the inadequacy
of parts of the work. For the present purpose, three or
four of these must suffice, as giving some indication of
the general level of artistic attainment in Greece about
the time when the first great sculptors arose.

The recent French excavations of Delphi have been
particularly rich in sculpture of this late archaic or
transitional period ; and among these sculptures none
are more remarkable than the frieze of the Treasury of
the Cnidians. The Treasury itself is a little gem of
Ionic architecture of the most ornate type, distinguished
by a crispness of carving and accuracy of form that is
to be matched in but few buildings of any age. Its
sculptures include a pedimental group on its principal

front as well as the frieze that goes all round it.    There
are considerable differences in style among these sculptures, showing probably the employment of various
hands in their execution, and even suggesting a doubt
as to whether they all belong to the same building.    The finest part is the frieze with scenes from
the battle of the gods and giants which ran along the
north side of the building ; a portion of this frieze, here
reproduced, includes a striking and original group
representing a figure in a chariot drawn by two lions
who seize and tear, with teeth and claws, a giant who
is borne down before their advance.    The figure in the
chariot, who wears a leopard-skin over long drapery, has
generally been identified as the Mother of the Gods,
though some prefer to recognise it as Dionysus.    Behind
it is Heracles, on so large a scale as to fill the whole
frieze ; he is protected by the lion-skin, which he
stretches out on his left arm, while with his right he
directs his spear against an antagonist who is seen
above the tails of the lions.    In front of the car
advance a pair of gods side by side, evidently Apollo
and Artemis, each drawing a bow ; just before them is
a fully armed warrior, running forward but turning his
head to look back.    From the wine-cup which supports
the crest of his helmet this figure has been identified
as Dionysus ; others see in him a giant who flies before

the advancing gods. Beyond him there advance to meet
the gods three giants in close array, and another lies
dead on the ground below them. On the shield of the
nearest giant is an inscription in a strange ornate
character, and containing the signature of the artist;
unfortunately his name is lost.[1] There is of course much
archaic technique to be seen in the execution of this
frieze. The warrior with the wine-cup on his helmet,
for example, shows the inability of an early artist to
realise a figure in the round ; his head is in exact profile
to the left, and his legs in profile to the right, while his
body is full-faced. Again, the lion tearing the giant,
though he is mainly seen in profile, has his scalp and
muzzle turned full-face so as to conform to the familiar
type of the lion mask which we find on coins and on
decorative works. Yet in spite of these defects the
variety and vigour of the composition is most impressive.
The contrast in the positions and weapons of the various
combatants, the life and energy of the whole, the way
in which the eye of the spectator is carried on from
group to group in alternating motion, all these show
mastery of the essential principles of design suitable
to such a frieze. And in spite of the usual inability or

[1] From the forms of letters, especially that of λ, it has been
suggested that the inscription is Argive ; but the same form occurs
on a Rhodian plate.

hesitation to represent any figure except in one or two
simple aspects, we see here and there a bold and even
a successful attempt at a different effect, as in the
upper part of the body of Apollo, which is almost in
true perspective.   Again, the giant who is being torn
by the lion, though he is to some extent put together
from inconsistent sections, yet shows a most vigorous
conception of a distorted figure; his arm, thrown across
the lion's mane, is a very bold attempt to realise a
portion of a figure in high relief in a new position.
There is of course some confusion and awkwardness in
these experiments; but, without them, it may be
doubted whether Myron, in the next generation, could
have made his marvellously distorted *Discobolus*.   It is
unfortunate that there is some doubt possible as to the
identification of this Treasury, for it would be instructive if we could know for certain whether the Cnidians
or the Siphnians are responsible for so characteristic a
monument of early sculpture.   It certainly has all the
richness and exuberance of the Ionic art of Asia Minor,
but combines with them a correctness of form and close
study of the human figure and limbs such as we rather
associate with the Dorian masters of athletic sculpture.
It is easy enough to explain this combination at Cnidus,
the Dorian city on the south-west corner of Asia Minor.
At Siphnos one would rather expect a connection with

PLATE VI

METOPE OF THE TREASURY OF THE ATHENIANS AT DELPHI; HERACLES
AND THE CERYNIAN STAG.  AFTER *FOUILLES DE DELPHES*, IV., XLI

*To face p.* 33

the neighbouring islands, especially those of Paros and Naxos, whence both the finest marbles and the skill to work them spread throughout Greece in the sixth century B.C.

As to another of the Delphian treasuries there is, happily, no such uncertainty. This is the one dedicated by the Athenians from the spoils of Marathon, and in all probability erected immediately after the battle in 490 B.C. Here the sculpture is restricted to the square metopes that alternate with the triglyphs of the Doric entablature all round the building; and the simpler and severer surroundings correspond in some degree to the style of the sculptures. The subjects are the exploits of Heracles and Theseus, most of them restricted to a simple group of two figures in combat or in conversation. The treatment of these subjects reminds us of the designs upon the Attic red-figured vases of the same period, and also of the decorative bronze figures that have been found on the Athenian Acropolis. We may take as an example one of the best preserved metopes, representing Heracles capturing the Cerynian stag. The hero sets his bent knee on the hind-quarters of the beast, and so forces it down to the ground, while his body bends over it, his hands doubtless seizing it by the horns. In the contorted position of the body thus produced, the sculptor has a splendid opportunity for

c

the display of his study of the muscles of the torso.
These are treated with great vigour, but in a somewhat
dry and conventional manner, the outlining of the
muscles on the front of the body, in particular, remind-
ing us of the regular pattern by which these are usually
drawn on vases. The head, too, with its short hair set
close to the scalp in minute curls, reminds us of the
technique of vase-painters and bronze-workers. But,
for all this resemblance to works of a decorative nature,
the bold modelling of the figure, and the skill with
which the twist of the body is rendered, make it worthy
of notice in its departure from the rigid 'frontality' of
early art. As a work made in the earlier part of the
life-time of Myron, it challenges comparison even with
his *Discobolus*. The position rendered offers an admirable illustration of Löwy's remark, that departure
from strict frontality is easiest in the case of a relief
figure in profile, and is in accordance with his principle
that the broadest aspect of every part of the figure is
selected. But when the result is as we see it here, there
is the greatest contrast to the crude efforts of primitive
sculptors in this direction.

The pedimental groups from the temple at Ægina,
which we now know to have been dedicated to the
goddess Aphæa, have long been amongst the most
familiar examples of early Greek sculpture. The name

Æginetan was indeed used by some ancient writers as almost equivalent to archaic, and though modern criticism shows more discrimination between the early schools, the Æginetan sculptures are still, perhaps, the most typical example of the work of the transitional period. The whole question of Æginetan art has been put in a new light by the recent investigations of Professor Furtwängler, which have shown that the old notion of the conventional arrangement of the pediments cannot be maintained. This old arrangement rested on no good authority, but was based on one out of several alternative suggestions sketched by Cockerell. It happened that this suggestion was followed in the arrangement of the sculptures, which had been found at Ægina in 1811, when they were restored by Thorwaldsen, and set up in the Munich museum ; and it has now become so familiar as to have acquired something like a prescriptive right. But it has no traditional authority ; it is merely the conjecture of archæologists who had not access to more than a portion of the data now available from more recent discoveries, from a closer study of what was found before, and from a comparison of other approximately contemporary compositions in sculpture and vase-painting. These new data, as collected by Professor Furtwängler in his " Ægina," have led him to propose a new arrangement which, though in many details it is still uncertain, is convincing in its main features, and must in all future treatises on Greek sculpture supersede the old.

It will be remembered that the groups from the Ægina pediments, as we are familiar with them in the Glyptothek at Munich, and in numerous reproductions, consist in each case of a central figure of the goddess Athena, and of a row of combatants on each side of her, all facing towards the centre of the composition, and appearing to be advancing in single file, though those at the back, spearmen and archers alike, are kneeling, so as to fit into the narrowing space confined by the line of the sloping roof. Much critical ingenuity has been spent upon the explanation of this arrangement; and the generally accepted theory has seen in it a kind of conventional perspective, the two parallel lines of fighters in the front rank on each side being opened out, so to speak, so that a spectator sees each one of them *in extenso*. Analogies for such an arrangement were sought in early Greek art, and even in such a composition as the frieze of the Parthenon, where, it was said, we see on the east front the head of the procession approaching from both ends simultaneously; and what we must really be supposed to see are the two sides of the same procession. Then the difference from Ægina would lie in the fact that, while both show a conventional expansion of two parallel lines, as if each were swung round on a pivot till the two were in one line, in the Parthenon frieze we are, so to speak, spectators from outside the procession in each case, in the Ægina pediments our imaginary position is in the space between the two lines. It seems worth while to dwell on this explanation, even if we now see reason to reject its applicability, because it is the result of some sound and accurate observations of early conventional perspective, as also many of the earlier criticisms of works like the *Apollo Belvedere* and the *Laocoon* are sound in principle, though the data on which they are based have been shown by fuller knowledge to be erroneous. Professor Furtwängler's investigations have, however, led to an arrangement of the figures which makes the earlier explanations inapplicable to the Ægina pediments. In the two pediments the figure of Athena retains its central position; on each side of her is a group of three figures similarly composed;—in the west pediment two standing combatants facing one another over a third, who had fallen between them; in the east pediment a spearman advancing upon a wounded adversary, who is in the act of collapsing into the outstretched arms of a comrade who stands forward ready to catch him. In each pediment there is an almost precisely similar group on each side of the central figure; and this

duplication, with slight variations, is very like what we
see on the Olympian pediments, and on other early
architectural sculptures.  There is, indeed, something
rather like it even in the pediments of the Parthenon;
but it is a very different thing from the rigid correspondence, figure to figure, of the old arrangement,
and gives us a much higher notion of the power and
elasticity of pedimental composition in the early fifth
century.  The central portion of the western pediment must suffice as an example of the whole.
Even here there is a certain amount that is conjectural; it has for some time been known that
there were probably four standing spearmen in this
pediment, though hitherto the pair on each side of the
central figure have not been set, as here, to face one
another.  Of the fallen warriors one has long been
placed either in or near the centre of the pediment; the
other is a new inference from somewhat scanty evidence,
mainly of one extant hand resting on the ground.  But
the similarity of these groups of three figures each, to
the groups of combatants which we constantly find on
Greek vases and reliefs, goes far to confirm the correctness of the new restoration.  Were the whole of the
sculpture a new discovery, there is hardly a doubt that
this restoration would have met with general acceptance; and a not unnatural prejudice in favour of a

restoration that has long been familiar should not make us hesitate to be guided by a study of the evidence old and new to what is certainly the most probable conclusion. At Ægina, as in the west pediment at Olympia, we can now see a development from the early type of pedimental group, which is broken up into a series of pairs of combatants, the chief pair in the middle, the rest balancing one another in number on the two sides, but showing no organic unity and little artistic adaptation to the space to be filled. The Æginetan artist has introduced two new elements, which contribute greatly to the effect of unity and concentration. The one is the quiet central figure, which itself does not form a part of any of the fighting groups; and the other is the balancing of groups of three figures, each of which contains a contrary motion within itself, and so gives a dynamic balance, so to speak, which is far more satisfactory to the eye than the mere static balance of single standing figures. This principle of motion within the various groups that make up the whole composition is one of very wide application in pedimental sculpture; it is not of course a new thing at Ægina, but it is for the first time realised and subordinated to the whole effect, and this change is as great an invention as the concentration of effort which we may see in Myron's *Discobolus*, as compared with earlier figures in

violent action.    Other details carry out the same principles in the subordinate parts of the pediments.    There
the kneeling spearmen in the west pediment face towards
the corners, and form a group with the fallen warriors
who occupy the extreme ends ; and so a motive is
gained for their position as well as variety in the
direction of their actions.    For these and other details,
and for the evidence on which the new reconstruction is
based, the reader must be referred to the exhaustive
treatment in Professor Furtwängler's " Ægina"; but
enough has been said to show that our notions of pedimental composition have been greatly modified and
enlarged by that work.

As regards the modelling of the figures themselves,
there is not so much to be added to our previous
knowledge from the new discoveries.    The Æginetan
style and the Æginetan type of figures are so clearly
marked that they can easily be recognised without the
help of external evidence.    The recognition depends
partly upon technical details, such as the rows of small
spiral curls in which the hair ends above the forehead,
and the form of the lips, which run up from a central
incision to a point at each end ; but such things as this
are easily imitated, and may be accidental.    What is
essential to the style consists rather in the proportion
of the body and in the modelling of torso and limbs.

Here, everything is concise, vigorous, and exact. The
figure is well knit together, broad at the shoulders, and
narrow at the waist ; the muscles are definitely planned
out and clearly outlined, on the conventional scheme
familiar on vases. The proportions give the impression
of a smaller and more compact figure than is suggested
by contemporary Attic work—for example, the statues
of the tyrannicides, Harmodius and Aristogiton. The
aims of the Æginetan sculptors seem less ambitious,
but are carried out with more certainty in execution.
There is room in early Greek sculpture for both tendencies—which may roughly be called realistic and
idealistic, though in a very different sense from that in
which those terms are used in connection with later
art. The characteristic type of the Æginetan school
evidently contains in itself the summary of long tradition and accurate observation, and shows us how the
knowledge of the human form was being acquired, so as
to make possible the later masterpieces of the fifth
century. Nor was the study of the Æginetan artists
confined to figures at rest. The various positions of
the battlefield, not only of combatants, but also of the
fallen and falling, and of those who press forward to
support the wounded, call for great variety of treatment ; and such variety of pose, to judge from literary
records, seems to have been a speciality with the

Æginetans, who sometimes represented athletes in positions of motion and activity, rather than of rest— for instance, a boxer sparring. The combatants and wounded men on the Ægina pediments thus anticipate in many ways the works of Myron and Cresilas. They show indeed many of the defects that are inherent in early work; the principal of frontality has always considerable influence, and in contorted bodies, such as that of the bearded warrior who reclines, wounded, in the corner of the east pediment, the upper and lower half of the body are modelled independently and inconsistently with each other; the sculptor is himself conscious of this, and contrives to hide the junction behind the arm or some other object. Another defect is that in the treatment of the face, particularly in expression, the Æginetan sculptors fall short of their excellence in rendering the body. This defect they share with other athletic schools. But their merits, in vigour and preciseness of work, and in variety of pose, are peculiarly their own, and form a most important contribution to the development of art. But the continuation of this development must be sought elsewhere. After the archaic period Ægina disappears politically before her rival Athens, and her artistic individuality is consequently lost also.

The other great series of architectural sculptures that

immediately precede the finest period are those of the
Temple of Zeus at Olympia. These are now so familiar
that it is needless to speak of them here at any length.
It is fortunate for us that the two sets of early architectural sculptures that are of the finest execution and
the most complete preservation should be those of
Ægina and Olympia. For the contrast between the
two is remarkable, and either alone would have given
us a very inadequate notion of the art that preceded
that familiar to us in the Parthenon. At Ægina, in
spite of any defects of detail, one feels that the art is
finished and finite. At Olympia, the sculptor is far
more ambitious; his conception is grander, his very
type of figure larger and more dignified; and for this
reason the unevenness of the execution, and its occasional
lapses into utterly inadequate work, are the more conspicuous. The choice of the subjects for the two pediments
is the most notable example of the selection of a quiet or
restful group for the front, and an active or violent one
for the back, an arrangement which is by some authorities
regarded as canonical, and which is certainly to be
observed in the pediments of many later temples. The
contrast, however, is nowhere so strongly marked as at
Olympia, and there it must be intentional. The eastern,
or front, pediment has in its middle five erect figures
standing side by side, with a chariot framing the

group, as it were, on each side where the space becomes narrower. The subject of the first or typical chariot race between Pelops and Œnomaus is here represented by the sacrifice to Zeus which preceded the actual contest, and which is evidently chosen by the artist, in preference to the race itself, as more suitable to a pediment, because of the possible concentration of its grouping, and also because it enabled him to get the effect of stability and repose which he regards as appropriate. The effect is monotonous, but remarkably successful in its dignity and calm ; being placed over the entrance to the cella, it was calculated to send the worshipper, fittingly prepared into the presence of the god. At the back of the temple the same considerations do not hold. Besides rigid simplicity, such as we find in the east pediment, the other effect best suited to the massive architectural frame is that of violent motion. And an extreme example of violent and even contorted motion is to be seen in the struggling group of Lapithæ and centaurs which fill the west pediment. Here, as at Ægina, there is a tendency for the composition to break up into groups of three, here consisting of a centaur, a Lapith woman, and a man coming to her rescue. But the central figure of Apollo, in the middle of the Olympian pediment, has a calm majesty far beyond that of Athena at Ægina, who

almost seems to take part in the fray. On the other
hand the groups of combatants are wilder in type and
bolder in composition; and this not merely because the
types followed were not so familiar; indeed, the
centauromachy was hardly less common as a subject
of early decorative art than combats between human
warriors; but because the sculptor of the Olympian
pediment has given free play to his imagination, and
so has produced a really new creation, not a mere
repetition of a stereotyped form. When we come to
consider the execution of the Olympian sculptures, we
find once more the greatest contrast to the Æginetan.
There all was "finished and finite," the artist had set
himself a task which was for the most part well within
his powers. His limitations are obvious, but, within
them, his work is complete and successful. At Olympia,
on the other hand, though there is much that is unsuccessful and even uncouth, we feel that the aims of
the sculptor are more ambitious if less attainable. The
majesty of the gods, the courage and resource of the
heroes, the agony of the victims, the keen interest of
the spectators—all are in some degree expressed; and
with an attempt at reality in the positions and expressions that is far removed from the conventions of earlier
work. It is true that the resources of the artist are
often insufficient to express all he has attempted. His

grouping is sometimes awkward, his symmetry forced. His knowledge of the human figure, especially of the athletic male figure, is excellent; but in female figures he is less successful, and his study of drapery has evidently been inadequate. Sometimes he succeeds by sheer sense of style and power of observation; in other cases his realism is timid or ineffective, because he has no tradition behind him. The modelling of the limbs through the drapery, above all in the female figures, is often defective. All these characteristics show us that the work must have been carried out by a body of artists such as one might expect to find at Olympia, more used to representations of the male than of the female form, and of the nude than of drapery. But the originality and nobility of design and conception that underlie the whole of the work transcend the convention under which the Æginetan masters had been content to work. Without Olympia, the wonderful advance from Ægina to the Parthenon would be unintelligible; but at Olympia we see at least an aspiration towards the power and majesty of design which was to be fulfilled in the work of Phidias.

It is not, however, in architectural sculptures only that a rapid progress is to be traced. For us they are invaluable, because of the comparative certainty with which they can be assigned a date and place. But the

PLATE VII

HEAD OF WARRIOR, PROBABLY ÆGINETAN, FROM THE ACROPOLIS
AT ATHENS

*To face p. 47*

great sculptors of Greece were not always or even
usually employed upon such works; it was indeed in
free statues that they had most scope for the exercise of
their individuality; and in the case of these statues,
which were actually made by their own hands, they
were less dependent on their surroundings and their
assistants. Two or three examples, however, must
suffice before we turn to the great masters; these two or
three are undoubtedly the work of eminent sculptors,
although it may not be possible for us to assert with
confidence who those sculptors were. The bronze head
of a man, evidently once helmeted, was found in the
excavations on the Athenian Acropolis. It has generally
been recognised as a product of Æginetan art; and we
know from inscriptions that some Æginetan sculptors,
including Onatas himself, were authors of works that
were dedicated on the Acropolis. The Æginetan
sculptures are the work of the same school, possibly of
the same artist, as this bronze head; but it has the
advantage of them, because it is in bronze, the material
in which the sculptors of Ægina and of other athletic
schools mostly worked. The head is very well preserved
but for the paste filling of the eyes. When this was
still intact, with its rendering of iris and pupil as we
see them in the *Charioteer of Delphi*, the expression
must have been wonderfully full of life and individuality.

There are indeed many archaic characteristics in the technique—the fine series of points along the edge of the hair, which were meant to show as a sort of fringe below the front of the helmet; the projecting ridge along the eye-brows; the sharp outlines and finely combed surface of the moustache and beard; the insufficient depth of the eye-sockets; above all, the somewhat crude archaic smile, which here resembles a "photographic expression," and so suggests that the artist has done his best to catch the transient if lively expression of his model. But the carefully rounded modelling of lips and cheeks gives reality to what would otherwise be a conventional mask. A head such as this shows us how the desire to give life to the work breaks through the conventions of archaic art. This may seem in contrast to the character of Æginetan work as we see it in the pediments; but we must remember that this head comes from a free statue, in all probability from a portrait statue. When we compare the restraint and dignity of style that mark especially the Peloponnesian schools of this period, a head like this, or some of the Attic statues of the same time, shows us another tendency which contributed to the perfection of the fifth century, the tendency towards the expression of life and even of mood. There is something genial and friendly about this head, such as we shall

PLATE VIII

BRONZE CHARIOTEER AT DELPHI

*To face p.* 49

hardly meet again in Greek art until the Hellenistic age.

The bronze *Charioteer of Delphi* is perhaps the most admirable example of transitional art that has come down to us. Here, in contrast to the exuberance of some contemporary work, we find the utmost simplicity and severity of style. There is nothing superfluous or accidental either in the modelling of the head and arm and feet, or of the folds of the drapery. This severity is enhanced by some archaic survivals in the technique— the clear definition of brows and lips, the lips inlaid in a different metal, the hair clinging so close to the scalp as hardly to affect its outline ; though the small curls, worked in the flat all over its surface, are most delicately rendered. The eyes still remain intact, with their paste filling, a soft brown in the iris, black in the pupil, and the white its natural colour ; and their effect, though extraordinarily life-like, has nothing staring about it, such as is sometimes seen in a similar technique in later Greek or modern times. This is partly owing to the way in which the pupils are shaded by the projecting margins of the bronze eye-sockets, which are cut into fine points to represent the eye-lashes. The first impression of severity, even of stiffness, which one may feel upon seeing this statue, gradually gives way to a feeling of its wonderful

D

combination of dignity and grace. The heavy folds
of the long tunic proper to a charioteer are studied with
the utmost care, whether they are gathered over the
shoulders and arms, or hang in parallel pleats from
the belt. The one arm and hand and the feet are
modelled with a perfection for which the careful study
of these parts in archaic art had prepared the way.
Their proportions are fine and graceful, and seem to
suggest an aristocratic type. The face has much resemblance, especially in profile, to the heads on Attic
vases of about the same period; but this must not be
too much insisted on as evidence for the authorship
of the statue. The relations of the various schools to
one another in the period immediately following the
Persian Wars were very close and very complicated. The
identification of this statue of a charioteer depends
partly upon the inscription that was engraved on its basis,
and that has been read as a dedication of the chariot
group by Polyzalos, the brother of Gelon and Hiero
of Syracuse. Many of the most famous sculptors of
Greece are recorded to have worked for this princely
family, among others Onatas and Glaucias of Ægina
and Calamis of Athens. After what we have seen of
Æginetan work, there can be no question of assigning
the *Charioteer of Delphi* to that school. The attribution
to Calamis is more tempting, and has actually been pro-

PLATE IX

HEAD OF BRONZE CHARIOTEER AT DELPHI

To face p. 50

posed in several quarters ; the grace and dignity of the
work and its Attic affinities favour such a suggestion.
But an erased and only partly legible inscription, which
has been superseded by that now visible, sets the
matter in a new light ; for it gives the name of the
original dedicator as ending in —ιλας, and it is almost
certain that this must be the end of the name of
Anaxilas, the well-known tyrant of Rhegium.[1]  If so
it is most probable, as has been pointed out by Professor
von Duhn, that the statue was by the most famous artist
of Rhegium, Pythagoras.   It would not perhaps be wise
to base any further inferences on such a succession of
probabilities as this, though one would like to associate
what is clearly a masterpiece with one of the greatest
of the recorded masters of the period.   But in any case
the *Charioteer* shows us at its best the sculpture which,
like Pindar's Odes, found its theme in the great victories
of the Olympian and Pythian games.   We evidently
see here no individual portrait, certainly not a representation of the crafty tyrant of Rhegium ; but a

1 This restoration of the name, and the consequent attribution
of the statue to Pythagoras, had occurred to me independently before
I saw Professor von Duhn's article in the " Athen. Mittheil." M.
Svoronos suggestion of Arcesilaus of Cyrene and the identification of
the statue as the *Battus* of Amphion is improbable chronologically ;
for Amphion's pupil Pison worked at the Ægospotami offering in
404 B.C. The whole matter is full of controversy.

figure of the ideal charioteer, youthful and alert, and of
a distinction and nobility of type which testifies to his
race. We know from the *Electra* of Sophocles that it
was thought fitting for a hero such as Orestes to drive
his own chariot, and certainly the driver, whoever he
was, is here immortalised together with the team
which his skill had guided to victory.

If the master who made the statue was Pythagoras
of Rhegium, we have at last some first-hand knowledge
of one of the three early sculptors who are classed
together by Brunn as the immediate forerunners of
Phidias; and this evidence must supersede earlier
conjectures as to the character of his art. It must,
however, be admitted that the evidence only amounts
to probability, not to certainty. As to Myron, the
second of the three, we have more information, so that
it is possible to assign him a separate chapter. Calamis,
the third, is another claimant to the authorship of the
*Charioteer*, mainly in virtue of his position as the leading
Attic artist of the time. In a book devoted to the
great sculptors of Greece, it might seem desirable to
give a chapter to Pythagoras and to Calamis. But
such chapters would have to be devoted mainly to the
discussion of literary evidence, and to the criticism of
various more or less probable theories. In the present
volume, our object is to deal only with artists who can

PLATE X

To face p. 53

RELIEF FROM THE "LUDOVISI THRONE"

actually be brought before us by their works; and for
that reason the *Charioteer*, as an original work of the
time of these sculptors, is of more value to us than
many descriptions of lost statues, or than many conjectural identifications of later copies. In it we can see
the spirit of the art of Greece, as it was in the days
of marvellously rapid progress that intervened between
the Persian invasion and the glory of Athens under
Pericles. To whatever individual master it be assigned,
it combines the severe dignity and nobility of type
that marks the Peloponnesian schools with a delicacy
and grace of execution and also with a power of ideal
treatment that are peculiarly Attic. The great artists
of this time, as we can see from the record of their
training and their commissions, did not work for their
own city alone, but for all Greece, and thus they
prepared the way for the time when Athens, under
Pericles and Phidias, was to draw to itself and embody
in its work all that was best and most characteristic in
Greek art as in Greek literature and philosophy.

Another work, this time a relief, may be quoted here
as representative of one at least of the tendencies of
this age of transition. This relief is on three sides of a
curious rectangular block of marble called the *Ludovisi
Throne* from its former owners; it is now in the
Museo delle Terme at Rome. On the two shorter

sides are two seated female figures, one fully draped, with a cloak drawn over her head and arms, and feeding a censer from a small box of incense; the other nude, and playing on the double flute. The larger relief, which is here reproduced, shows a slender girlish figure arising out of the ground, and being helped up by two draped female figures, each of whom places one hand under the shoulder of the rising figure, while her other hand supports a piece of drapery that falls in graceful folds across the front. The subject of this group has been much disputed. Perhaps the most popular explanation is that it represents Aphrodite arising from the sea. It would, however, be more in accordance with mythological probability, and also with the evident reference to the season in the two figures on the sides of the throne, to recognise here either Persephone or the earth goddess arising out of the ground, a favourite subject upon Attic vases. The originality and expressive grace of the composition, the upward aspiration of the central figure, the evident care with which every detail of modelling and of drapery has been worked out, all these are characteristic of the transitional age; no less so are the technical defects of the execution, the too masculine proportions of the central figure, the placing of the breasts right at the side, the want of harmony between the drapery

and the limbs which it sometimes envelops entirely,
sometimes reveals in a manner untrue to its own texture.
Some of these qualities, both good and bad, are more
proper to drawing than to sculpture, and doubtless show
the influence of the sister art. This influence, especially
in the days when Polygnotus was painting his great
frescoes at Athens and at Delphi, probably contributed
much to the sum of fifth-century art. In the case of
this *Ludovisi Throne* we are again uncertain as to the
exact local school to which it should be assigned. But
the poetical imagination and power of pictorial composition which we can see in such a relief as this supplement the more sculptural qualities which we noticed
in the *Charioteer of Delphi*, as exemplifying the tendencies of the art that was, in the next generation, to
produce the sculptures of the Parthenon.

# CHAPTER III

## MYRON

ACCORDING to the common verdict of antiquity, Myron was the earliest of the great masters of Greek sculpture. That is to say, he was the earliest sculptor whose works appeared, even to critics who were familiar with the whole range of later art, to be admirable alike for the boldness and originality of their design and the skill of their execution, and who was spoken of in the same breath with Polyclitus and Lysippus, with Phidias and Praxiteles. Nor was this high estimate of his excellence confined to those who prefer the uncouth but promising attempts of art in its infancy to the masterpieces of its prime. Quintilian, who charges such critics with an affectation of superiority as connoisseurs, himself declares that to find fault with the *Discobolus* argues a lack of appreciation of art.

Happily, we are not compelled to judge the work of Myron on hearsay evidence, since we possess copies of some of his statues, in one case at least giving an

excellent notion of the original. But the testimony of
ancient writers is useful, because it shows us that the
prominent position among sculptors now held by
Myron is not due merely to the accident that his
works have survived while those of his rivals and
contemporaries are lost. It is true that there were
sculptors before Myron, and that they have not entirely
lacked a chronicler; and that his contemporaries,
Pythagoras and Calamis, though they did not equal his
fame, are spoken of by some ancient critics in terms
which tantalise us with the beauties they imply. But,
however fascinating the delicate grace of Calamis [1]
would probably have proved to a taste that prefers the
Pre-Raphaelite painters to all later art, there is little
doubt that Myron's originality, vigour, and technical
excellence would in any case have vindicated for him
the same estimation among modern critics which he
commanded in the ancient world.

We know but little about Myron's life. He was a
native of Eleutheræ, a town on the frontier of Attica
and Bœotia. To judge from the list of his works and
the places where they were set up, he must, in his
prime, have enjoyed a reputation throughout Hellenic

---

[1] It is assumed here that we possess no statue certainly by Calamis. The French excavators were inclined to attribute the *Delphi
Charioteer* to him; but there are various theories about this statue.

lands; statues of athletic victors from his hand were to
be seen at Olympia and at Delphi.   But several of his
most famous works were in Athens, and it is probable
that his artistic career was mainly associated with that
city.   He is recorded, however, to have been a pupil of
the Argive sculptor Ageladas, who was for a long time
the acknowledged leader of the Peloponnesian school of
athletic sculpture; and it is said that his fellow-pupils
were Phidias and Polyclitus.   The story has met with
much criticism, for Phidias was probably younger than
Myron, and the career of Polyclitus, though it barely
overlaps that of Myron, lasts to a much later date.
The error in chronology need not, however, discredit
the whole story.   Nothing is more probable than that
Myron, as a young man especially interested in the
sculpture of athletic subjects, should have studied
under the recognised master of this branch of art; and
at the beginning of the fifth century, the time of
Myron's youth, there is abundant evidence that the
various local schools were having considerable influence
upon one another, and in particular that the influence
of Argos was being felt in Athens.   Even if the tale
rests on no good authority as to the fact, it may be
based on a sound artistic criticism, made by men who
were familiar with works that are now lost to us or
only identifiable by conjecture.

The dates of Myron's artistic career can be fixed
with certainty by the Olympiads of the victors whose
statues he made; Lycinus won in 448 B.C., and Timan-
thes in 456; Ladas probably in 476; but so famous an
athlete may have had a statue set up in his honour
some years after the event. The traditional date given
by Pliny which makes Myron a contemporary of
Polyclitus is evidently wrong. His son Lycius was
employed on an important public commission, the
statues set up by the knights of Athens at the entrance
to the Acropolis, about 446 B.C. We must, therefore,
assign the artistic activity of Myron himself to the first
half of the fifth century. His early manhood must
have coincided with the period of the Persian wars.
But Eleutheræ ranked as Bœotian until 460 B.C., and
the Bœotians had no share in the victories that freed
Greece from the barbarian invader. Myron's sym-
pathies were probably with Athens; but no work of
his is recorded which has any reference, direct or
indirect, to the events that had so great a share in the
inspiration of Phidias.

Athletic sculpture, as it was understood before the
time of Myron, had already made considerable progress.
The days were past when a rigid and erect figure, its
left leg advanced in the conventional Egyptian pose,
its arms firmly fixed to its sides, the two sides of its

body exactly matching, might serve alike for athlete
or Apollo, for an ornament to the precinct of a god or
for a monument over a tomb.  The sculptors of the
Argive school, though they still preferred a position of
rest, had learnt to ease the stiffness of the standing
figure, and to bend its median line into a graceful
curve, by inclining the head slightly to one side and by
throwing the weight of the body on one leg, so that one
hip was higher than the other, and a corresponding
variety was introduced into the lines of the muscles on
the chest and abdomen.   And, moreover, by a constant
sequence of study of nature in detail, and by a school
tradition which ensured that knowledge or observation
once gained was not lost again, they had won a
familiarity with the visible forms of body and limbs
which found expression by means of a skilful and
accurate technique.  All this Myron could learn from his
master Ageladas; but the general tendency of the Argive
school was undoubtedly towards a somewhat stiff and
formal perfection, such as found its most characteristic
example in the works of Polyclitus.  The more exu-
berant side of Myron's genius would have been more in
sympathy with the attempts of the Æginetans to
represent figures in vigorous or violent action ; the
most familiar example of such actions is to be seen in
the battle groups that have survived to our day in the

PLATE XI

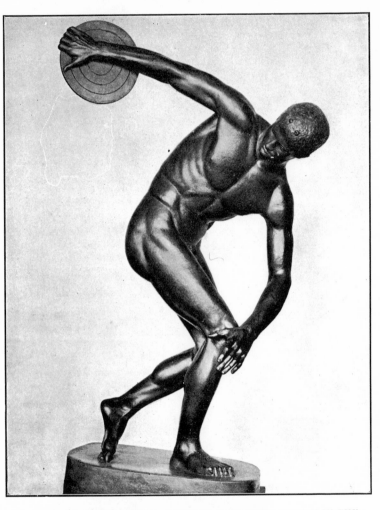

DISCOBOLUS, AFTER MYRON; BRONZED CAST FROM STATUE IN THE
VATICAN; HEAD FROM MASSIMI STATUE

To face p. 61

pediments of the temple; but the Æginetan sculptors
also made single figures of the same kind, for instance,
the famous boxer Glaucus in the act of sparring
(σκιαμαχῶν). Such works may well be regarded as the
direct predecessors of the *Discobolus*. In Athens, too,
statues in strong motion were not unknown; the
tyrannicides Harmodius and Aristogiton were represented in the midst of their impetuous onset upon
Hipparchus, and their statues, still preserved in copies
to the present day, show an astonishing dash and
vigour of invention.

It was no new departure in art for Myron to represent an athlete practising the exercise in which he
excelled. His great attainment, as exemplified by the
*Discobolus*, was the choice of a subject and a moment
that was suitable to representation in sculpture. He
appears to have been the first to realise the principle,
never afterwards violated in Greek sculpture of the best
period, that a statue or a sculptural group must be
complete in itself, must possess a certain unity and
concentration, so as to attract and contain the interest
of the spectator within the work itself, and not to
direct it to other extraneous objects, nor even to allow
it to wander away. The group of the tyrannicides, for
all its vigour, will not stand this test; the two advancing heroes imply the presence of the tyrant against

whom they advance, and thus the central point both
of composition and of interest is placed outside the
actual group; the result, from the artistic point of
view, is almost as unsatisfactory to the eye as if the
apparent centre of gravity of the group lay outside its
base; there is an unstable equilibrium, so to speak, in
the realm of artistic composition as well as in that of
gravity. A similar criticism applies, though in a less
degree, to the well-known statuette, in the Louvre, of
Heracles striking with his club, or to the statue, known
to us only by description, of *Glaucus sparring*; whether
he was thought of as facing an antagonist, or merely
punching a ball or pad, something is implied outside
the statue itself to complete the action.

In the *Discobolus*, the self-contained completeness in
the action finds its expression and counterpart in the
lines of the composition itself. It may be, as Quintilian
says, laboured and contorted, but the result is not, as
might have been expected, restless in effect or tiring to
the eye, because every part is in harmony with the
whole, and the eye is carried on by an easy and pleasing
succession of outlines round the whole contour of the
figure. Beside this excellence of artistic composition,
the clever choice of the right moment for representation
and of an athletic exercise in which such a moment
occurs must also be allowed their merit. The disc or

PLATE XII

DISCOBOLUS, AFTER MYRON; RESTORED CAST; TORSO
FROM STATUE IN MUSEO DELLE TERME; HEAD FROM
MASSIMI STATUE

quoit was not aimed at any mark, but merely hurled
as far as possible in a given direction, as in the modern
competitions of putting the weight or throwing the
hammer. Therefore there was no need for the eye of
the competitor to be turned towards a distant goal, but
the head could follow the motion of the arm that
swung the quoit, the position of the feet sufficing to
define the direction of the throw. A false restoration,
which makes the thrower turn his head toward this
direction, not only produces a painful and even impossible attitude, but also destroys the harmony of
the composition, by breaking in upon the system of
concentric curves in which every member of the body
follows the swing of the extended arm.

The extant copies of the *Discobolus* are numerous,
but the one which stands out conspicuous among them
for the care and accuracy of its execution and its evident
fidelity to the original is that in the Palazzo Lancelotti
at Rome; it was formerly in the Palazzo Massimi alla
Colonna, and therefore is sometimes referred to as the
*Massimi Discobolus*. It is not only as preserving the
correct pose of the original that this copy is of value to
us: in the type of face, in treatment of hair, in the
rendering of the muscles and the surface of the body, it
differs greatly from other copies, and we can hardly
doubt that the difference brings it nearer to the work

of Myron himself.[1] In the case of other copies, so many later elements have been introduced that it is difficult to realise that they are derived from a statue made in the earlier years of the fifth century; apart from the external evidence, and the descriptions of Lucian and Quintilian, the original of these would hardly have been assigned to so early a date. But with the *Lancelotti Discobolus* it is otherwise. The form of the head shows early Attic proportions, especially in the long oval of the face. The modelling is simple and severe, the treatment of the hair conventional, especially in the outline above the forehead; the expression is calm and impassive, and has no relation to the vigorous action of the figure. In the body and limbs the various muscles and masses of flesh are clearly defined, and their outlines are indicated with a distinctness that is partly conventional, and that reminds us of the drawing of the muscles of the torso upon Attic vases of the severe type. In early sculpture, both in bronze and marble, and especially in early Attic sculpture, we often see the muscles outlined by incised grooves; but

1 The illustration (Pl. XI.) is taken from a cast in which the head of the *Massimi Discobolus* is added to the Vatican torso, and the whole cast then bronzed over. The other illustration (Pl. XII.) shows a recently discovered and very fine copy, now in the Museo delle Terme at Rome. The torso only was found, but the head and legs are restored from the Massimi and other copies.

PLATE XIII

HEAD OF MASSIMI DISCOBOLUS

To face **p.** 64

they are indicated by drawing rather than by modelling.
In the *Discobolus*, on the other hand, the clear lines of
demarcation are not inconsistent with a correct and
skilful modelling of the surface. The effect is perhaps
somewhat dry, and suggests the appearance of a man in
hard training, and even the tension of muscles that
would not be exerted at the moment of action is portrayed. But what convention is left is so thoroughly
harmonised with the results of fresh observation as to give
the impression of a living body, and to justify the criticism applied to Myron by ancient critics, that he " could
all but enclose in bronze the very life of men and beasts."

Before considering further the artistic character of
Myron, which is known to us chiefly from the study of
the copies of the *Discobolus*, it seems advisable to
review briefly what other literary evidence we possess
as to his work, and what other extant statues may be
attributed to him or associated with him. The best
known of these is the statue of *Marsyas* in the Lateran
Museum at Rome. This statue is restored as a dancing
satyr, but it has been identified, by the help of representations on vases, reliefs, and coins, as a copy of the
*Marsyas* who was associated with *Athena* in a famous
group by Myron, seen by Pausanias on the Acropolis
at Athens. The goddess had thrown down in disgust
the flutes which she could not play without unseemly

E

distortion of her features; and *Marsyas* approached to
pick them up. The moment chosen by the sculptor is
that in which the satyr starts back in sudden astonish-
ment, whether at the flutes themselves or at the
approach of the goddess; unfortunately, the extant
copies of the group vary so much that it is impossible
to attain any certainty on this point, but the motive of
the figure of *Marsyas* is evident enough.   In some ways
it offers a counterpart to the *Discobolus*, since it represents the moment of rest immediately succeeding violent
motion; but in the *Discobolus* this moment is the
preparation for still more vigorous action to succeed,
while in the *Marsyas* there is no succeeding action
implied.   In this respect the subject is less con-
spicuously fitting for sculpture; but we must remark
that the *Marsyas* is part of a group, and was not
intended to be complete in itself.[1]

No copy of the *Marsyas* is to be compared in quality
with the *Lancelotti Discobolus*.   The Lateran statue,
however, shows a good deal that is characteristic of
Myron, especially in the dry, sinewy forms of the body
and the clearly outlined muscles.   The mask-like,
satyric face also resembles that of the *Discobolus* in the
absence of any attempt to represent an excitement or
emotion corresponding to the violence of the action.

[1] The *Athena* has perhaps been identified ; *see* p. 72.

PLATE XIV

MARSYAS, AFTER MYRON; BRONZE STATUETTE IN THE
BRITISH MUSEUM          *To face p. 67*

The deep furrows on his brow and on his cheeks
may seem at first sight to contradict this statement.
But they belong to the physical type of the satyr,
with its half-bestial character, rather than to any
momentary expression. It is true that there is more
expression in the head from the Barracco collection,
identified by M. Collignon[1] as an ancient copy of the
*Marsyas;* but even if this identification be accepted,
the copy need bear no nearer relation to the original
by Myron than does the well-known bronze statuette in
the British Museum, which is merely a Hellenistic
variation on the subject devised by Myron, but has
nothing Myronic either in its composition or in its
execution. We have seen in the case of the *Discobolus*
also how the face is modified in ancient copies to suit
the taste of a later age.

Literary evidence about a sculptor is, as a rule, of
little practical use, except so far as it can be brought
into relation with extant sculptures that are either
derived from his works or show his influence. In the
case of Myron, however, as an artist of the transition
from archaism to freedom, the ancient criticisms that
are recorded are more explicit and definite, and so have
a value for us. Such are the statements that he still

1 "Mélanges d'Arch. et Hist. de l'École française de Rome,"
x. 1890, ii,

kept to the archaic rendering of the hair, that he devoted his attention to the forms of the body and did not give expression to emotion or passion (*animi sensus*), that his art had more variety than that of Polyclitus, that he enlarged the field within which true observation of nature was possible. The saying that he "could all but enclose in bronze the very life of men and beasts" has already been quoted. In addition to such general criticisms we find many epigrams referring to particular statues, especially the famous *Heifer* and the *Ladas*. The *Heifer*, indeed, became a commonplace for the exercise of poetical ingenuity in Hellenistic and Roman times; but the numerous epigrams tell us little or nothing about the work itself, except by vaunting its extraordinary truth to life, which is said to have been such as to deceive both herdsmen and cattle. A perfection like this in the representation of beasts is by no means improbable at the very beginning of the age of freedom in art; it may be paralleled by the unrivalled skill of Calamis in the rendering of horses. But it is useless, in the absence of any figure of an animal that can be referred with any probability to Myron, to pursue this matter any further. The two epigrams about the *Ladas*, on the other hand, tell us rather more about the statue. Its fame was partly due to the picturesque tale about *Ladas*, and how his victory in the long foot-race cost him his life. He did not indeed, as is sometimes said, fall dead at the goal; but he never recovered from the strain of the race, and died on his way home to Argos. The two epigrams run as follows:

"Like as thou wast in life, Ladas, breathing forth [1] thy panting soul, on tip-toe, with every sinew at full strain, such hath Myron wrought thee in bronze, stamping on thy whole body thy eagerness for the victor's crown of Pisa."

" He is filled with hope, and you may see the breath caught on his lips from deep within his flanks; surely the bronze will leave its pedestal and leap to the crown. Such art is swifter than the wind."

There can be little doubt from these two epigrams that Ladas must have been represented as a runner at full speed approaching the goal; and, even after allowing for what is rhetorical in the description, we must infer that Myron embodied in this statue the conception of the athlete that we see in the story and the epigrams—the long-distance runner in the eager tension of his final spurt, straining wind and limb to the utmost, and calling up all the reserves of his strength and endurance for the concentrated effort from which he was

---

[1] I read φυσῶν θυμὸν for φεύγων, which is nonsense. Φεύγων Θυμόν, "flying from Thymus," does not seem to me so probable a reading. ΦΤΓΩΝ is a very easy corruption for ΦΤΓΩΝ, and the E would naturally be added by a scribe to correct the scansion.

never destined to recover. The technical difficulty of
rendering in bronze a runner at full speed is one from
which the sculptor of the *Discobolus* may not have
shrunk. How far the attempt was successful from the
artistic point of view we cannot now judge. It is, however, to be noted that the eagerness mentioned in the
first epigram is said to be stamped on the whole body,
not expressed in the face, though doubtless the panting
breath may also have been indicated, at least by half
opening the lips. This is quite in accordance with the
impression as to Myron's work which we derive from the
*Discobolus*; here too, it is the expression of the vigour
and action of physical life rather than of emotional or
spiritual character that is the aim and attainment of
the sculptor. The contrast between this and the eager
charioteer of Scopas on the Mausoleum[1] shows the wide
gulf between the two artists.

A mere enumeration of Myron's other recorded works
gives us some indication of the subjects he preferred.
The attention of Pausanias was especially attracted by
a statue of *Erechtheus* at Athens, and by a statue of
*Perseus* on the Athenian Acropolis. This hero was
represented just after his exploit against Medusa. The
subject recalls the *Perseus* of Benvenuto Cellini, which,
indeed, has something Myronic about it; but it would

1 Page 205.

be unsafe to infer any similarity in its treatment.[1]
Various statues of gods were attributed to Myron;
Pausanias especially praises his *Dionysus* on Mount
Helicon.    Other statues of gods made by him were a
*Hecate* at Ægina, an *Apollo* at Ephesus, another at
Agrigentum, and a colossal group of *Zeus, Athena, and
Heracles* in the Heræum at Samos; at least two other
statues are recorded.    He also made several statues of
athletic victors, besides the famous *Ladas*, including
representations of almost every form of contest, the
chariot-race amongst others.    The list of his works is
concluded by two that have given rise to a good deal
of controversy.    One is a famous marble statue of a
drunken old woman, expressly attributed by Pliny to
the great Myron.    Several copies of a statue of this
subject are known; but, so far as it is possible to judge
from their style, they do not seem to go back to an
original of so early a date.    The later modifications of
the *Marsyas*, however, teach us caution in this matter;
Myron may have made the statue from which all are
ultimately derived, though it is not easy for us to conjecture how he would have treated such a subject.
Finally, we have the mysterious *pristæ*, which have

[1] Furtwängler's attempt to attribute the head of Perseus in the
British Museum to Myron seems to me unsuccessful; Dr. A. S. Murray
seems nearer the mark in saying the original must be sought in the
fourth century.

been variously interpreted as sea-monsters, sawyers, or
players at see-saw, not to speak of various emendations,
such as Loeschcke's pyctas—boxers.  Discussions of
such matters, though they offer scope for the ingenuity
of the critic, do not usually contribute in any high degree
to our knowledge of the artist.  But the mere list of
works attributed to Myron suffices to show his originality
and his versatility.  His subjects, it is true, are mainly
of an athletic type; but his treatment of athletes was
far removed from the conventional; in the case of *Ladas*,
for example, he seems to have used the theme as a pre-
text for making one of the most striking and original
statues of ancient times.  It is significant also that
among his statues of the gods that of *Dionysus* should
be selected by Pausanias for special praise; such a
statue of the god of wine and of bacchic frenzy can
hardly have been commonplace.  The chief defect in
the list of his works lies in the comparative absence
of female figures; apart from the *Hecate* on Ægina we
only hear of two statues of *Athena*, both in groups: the
one associated with the *Marsyas* has been conjecturally
identified in a statue which resembles that on the
coins; the reconstituted group may be seen in the
*Jahrbuch* of the German Institut, 1908, the statue
in *Oester. Jahreshefte*, 1909.  Its effect is not very
satisfactory, and may explain the variation which we

PLATE XV

MARBLE STATUETTE OF HERCULES

To face p. 73

find in the figure of the goddess in other copies of
the group. There were, as we have seen, at least
three statues of *Heracles* in the list of his works ; and
this fact seems to justify us in connecting with him a
statuette of *Heracles* which evidently shows affinity
with his style. This statuette, as was to be expected
from its subject, shows a heavier and more massive type
of figure than the *Discobolus;* but the clear and dry
rendering of the muscles is similar, and also the close-set
curls of hair and beard, which, however, stand out
rather more strongly from the head. This is quite
in accordance with the rendering of Heracles in Attic
vases ; the close-set, projecting curls are almost a
typical adjunct of great physical strength. But the
outline of both hair and beard is strictly defined. The
position and general character of the work are remarkable. The hero is represented at rest, his right
hand leaning on his club, his lion-skin on his left arm :
his pose, especially the gentle inclination of his head
towards the left, suggests something of weariness. The
type of the weary Heracles, the hero overwhelmed with
his labours, is a common one in later art, and is especially
associated with Lysippus. It is most interesting to find
an anticipation of it in a work which must be about a
century and a half earlier, and which suggests association with Myron. The connection is confirmed by a

colossal head of Heracles in the British Museum, which
shows the same characteristics, and which Furtwängler,
in spite of some later modifications, referred to a
Myronic original. Nor is it improbable that the
sculptor who could, in his *Ladas*, express the enthusiasm
of the effort that cost the victor his life, should also
have created the conception of the hero who, in his
moments of rest, is oppressed by the consciousness of
his labours. Both alike are phases of the psychology
of the athlete, and thus peculiarly suited to Myron's
predilections.

But, after all, it is the *Discobolus* and the *Marsyas*
on which we chiefly depend for our knowledge of
Myron ; and with their help we can associate with him
a certain number of extant works in our museums ;
though it is not likely that any of them are originals
from his hand, some of them may be attributed to his
pupils, and others may be copied more or less directly
from his works. The first place where one naturally
looks for his influence is in the great mass of architectural sculptures that was made in Athens during the
generation next following his own, by the set of artists
among whom his son was working. The pediments and
the frieze of the Parthenon are so dominated by the
personality of one great master—who can be no other
than Phidias himself—that it is not easy to distinguish

PLATE XVI

METOPE OF THE PARTHENON; LAPITH AND CENTAUR

To face p. 75

different hands or variations of style in their execution.
But with the metopes it is otherwise. Some of these
show an angularity and some an awkwardness of pose,
and a hard and dry rendering of the muscles that is
distinctly archaic, and that recalls the defects and
mannerisms, though not the excellence, of Myron's
work. Such mannerisms are just what a pupil or
imitator might copy, while he missed the higher qualities
of his master's attainments; but at the same time it
must be admitted that the peculiarities that we have
noticed may have belonged to Myron's age rather than
to himself. Even if this were the case, however, it was
probably his reputation that served to perpetuate and
to transmit them. Besides these, the least successful of
the Parthenon metopes, there is another set, intermediate in character between them and the most
advanced in style, which last we may attribute to the
influence of Phidias himself. This intermediate set are
characterised by great vigour in composition, by study
of balance in pose, and by familiarity with athletic
devices, while it still retains the hard and dry treatment
of muscles, especially in the torso. It therefore comes
closer in every way to the work of Myron himself;
perhaps we may be justified in attributing at least
these metopes to a pupil of Myron—possibly to his
son Lycius. The spirited treatment of the centaur would

well suit an artist who was selected to make the equestrian statues of the Athenian knights set up at the entrance to the Acropolis. The metopes of the Theseum, as has generally been recognised, have an affinity with the earlier metopes of the Parthenon, and may be attributed to the same influence; they show the same delight in athletic motives, and the same predilections for angular and even uncouth positions.[1] We cannot, indeed, learn much from these architectural sculptures about Myron, but we can see in them the reflection of his style, and trace his influence upon his contemporaries and successors.

To pass from such architectural work to independent statues, the head of the *Massimi Discobolus* has enabled us to recognise a whole series of heads as Myronic, or at least as showing Myron's influence. This series has been traced, with the help of a succession of links, all probably of Attic workmanship, right through to the head of the *Hermes* of Praxiteles. The most familiar of intermediate examples is a beautiful statue of an athlete standing and pouring oil from his right hand, raised above his head, into his left, which is held in front of his body. This athlete was attributed by Brunn to

[1] I see no reason for the preference of Furtwängler and others for Critius as the source of the athletic influence in the metopes of Parthenon and Theseum. It seems to me that they have far less in common with the *Tyrannicides* than with the *Discobolus.*

PLATE XVII

DIOMED WITH THE PALLADIUM; STATUE IN MUNICH

*To face p. 77*

Myron himself. It is now generally regarded as the work of a later Attic artist who fell under his influence, perhaps Alcamenes.[1] Here not only the head but the whole motive and pose of the figure are intermediate between Myron and Praxiteles, and help one to realise —what we might easily miss if we had no intermediate link—that there is an affinity between the two, though a whole century of rapid development intervenes.

Another set of statues, which has been with much ingenuity and a high degree of probability assigned by Furtwängler to Cresilas, also shows distinct traces of the influence of Myron. Among these is the well-known portrait of Pericles, of which there is a good copy in the British Museum, and the statue of *Diomed with the Palladium*, which has survived in several copies; to these Furtwängler would add the wounded Amazon of the Capitoline type, in which the pain of the wound is made the motive of the whole figure, and the pathetic effect is most skilfully attained. It would be out of place here to discuss the work of Cresilas, but these works are quoted because they perhaps help us to trace a further development of the style of Myron. Intermediate in character between them and the rather impassive head of the *Massimi Discobolus*, but extremely similar to the latter in type, is a head in the Palazzo Riccardi at

[1] Furtwängler suggests Lycius ; "Masterpieces," p. 296.

Rome.[1] This may well be a copy of a work of Myron's later years. It has the same closely curling hair as the *Discobolus*, the same marked eyelids, the same rather full lips, and a similar shape of face. There is, however, far more attempt at expression, though it is not in this respect as advanced as the *Diomed*. Even if we do not follow Furtwängler in the problematic series of identifications which he adds, we may admit the truth of his inference that the Riccardi head should make us modify the opinion, recorded by ancient writers, that Myron, though excellent in rendering physical life, was deficient in the expression of mental or emotional qualities. Doubtless it was for the first that he was most famous among the later Greeks; but we should be limiting unduly the scope of his originality if we altogether denied him the other.

[1] This head has long been recognised as Myronic. *See* Friedrichs-Wolters, "Bausteine," No. 458. A similar, but narrower, head is in the Ince-Blundell collection ; another at Ny Karlsberg.

PLATE XVIII

"RICCARDI HEAD"; STYLE OF MYRON

*To face p.* 78

# CHAPTER IV

## PHIDIAS

THE estimate which sets Phidias in the foremost place among Greek sculptors is probably a just one; but it has not always met with acceptance. For example, the canon of sculpture from which Pliny borrows much of his criticism, and which was probably derived from a writer of the Sicyonian School, regards Phidias rather as a forerunner of Polyclitus, as a pioneer in the art which Polyclitus brought to the highest perfection. The causes that have led in modern times to a general acknowledgment of the supremacy of Phidias are two-fold. In the first place, the description of his colossal statues of the gods, and the enthusiastic appreciation of them, especially by later rhetorical writers, has impressed the imagination of modern students; and, in the second place, the extraordinary excellence of the Elgin marbles has met with so universal recognition among artists and critics as to place the sculptor to whose influence they must be attributed in a position

79

apart from all rivalry. Curiously enough, the two reasons seem quite independent of each other ; the ancient writers who refer to Phidias are thinking of his separate statues, especially of his colossal gold and ivory *Zeus* and *Athena;* and of these we either possess no copies at all, or copies so unsatisfactory as to transmit to us but the faintest reflection of their originals, while the Elgin marbles were, to the Greeks, merely architectural sculptures, not thought worthy of mention by any ancient writer except Pausanias, who dismisses them in a few words. It follows from the fragmentary and unsatisfactory nature of the evidence that our know-ledge of Phidias is mainly derived from a series of infer-ences or even of assumptions. The facts which can be ascertained may thus be summarised. We can gather, from various indications, a fair notion of the attainments of sculpture in Athens about the middle of the fifth cen-tury; and we can see, in the sculptures of the Parthenon, executed just after that date, new elements of striking originality ; we find a mastery free from exaggeration in the treatment of the nude, a marvellous grace and delicacy, yet absence of anything like affectation or over-refinement in the rendering of drapery, above all a breadth and nobility of conception alike in the type and pose of the figures, in the composition of the groups, and in the ideas that are expressed ; and all these are

far beyond anything that has gone before. So far as
mere technical skill is concerned, this advance may
be partly attributed to the wonderful progress among
Greek sculptors, and especially in the Athenian school,
that is the characteristic of the age. But it is no
more possible to attribute the pediments and frieze of
the Parthenon to such general progress than it is
possible to attribute the *Prometheus* or the *Agamemnon*
to a general advance in literary skill and appreciation.
In both cases alike we must see the work of individual
genius; and it is impossible to suggest as the author
any other than Phidias, who made the colossal statue
within the temple, and who was associated with Pericles
in the direction of all the artistic activity that was at
this time expended upon the Athenian Acropolis.

Apart from architectural sculptures, we also find a
change in the statues of the gods of the same period,
and may well infer that this change was due, mainly or
in part, to the influence of Phidias, and to the colossal
masterpieces that were regarded in ancient times as his
representative works. Here, however, we are on more
difficult ground; for Phidias was surrounded by a group
of sculptors of similar aims and tendencies—Agoracritus,
Alcamenes, and others, whose work was sometimes hard
to distinguish from his own; and it is uncertain how
much we must concede to the personal qualities of these

other masters. They must undoubtedly have fallen under his influence, and, with him, they embodied those ideals of the chief gods which were accepted as canonical by all later generations. If, however, even ancient critics sometimes found it difficult to distinguish what was his from what was theirs, this only shows the more clearly how completely they were dominated by his artistic personality. But the colossal statues which they made have in no case survived, with the exception of a few fragments; and although we may infer something from the reflection of these great works in all later art, the Elgin marbles still remain the most trustworthy record of the work of Phidias.

The date of Phidias' birth can only be inferred from the fact that the figure on the shield of the *Athena Parthenos*, said to be a portrait of himself, was that of a bald-headed old man, yet of a man still in the full vigour of his strength, since he was taking an active part in the battle of Greeks and Amazons. The statue was dedicated in 438 B.C.; and it seems a reasonable inference that Phidias was born about the end of the sixth century, a date that fits in very well with what we know otherwise as to his artistic career. As a boy, he would remember the victory of Marathon, and the glory it gave to his people of Athens and to their faithful allies the Platæans, for whom also, in later years, he

PLATE XIX

"STRANGFORD SHIELD," IN BRITISH MUSEUM

*To face p.* 82

was to make a statue commemorating their share in the
battle. As a young man, he must have fought at
Salamis and at Platæa ; it was perhaps a reminiscence
of his valour on these occasions that led him to place
himself as a combatant upon the shield of the *Athena
Parthenos*, for the victories over the Persians were commemorated partly by trophies erected from the spoil of
the enemy, partly by the more indirect reference which
made the battles of the Greeks against Centaurs or
Amazons a favourite theme in the art of the fifth century.
This personal commemoration reminds us of the epitaph
of Æschylus, who counted his valour against the Persians
at Marathon the event of his life most worthy to be
recorded on his tomb. The pupilage of Phidias belongs
to the time of the Persian wars. He is said to have worked
as a painter also in his youth ; the knowledge he gained
would be most useful to him in designing the ornamentation and accessories of his colossal statues, and in
supervising the work of other painters, such as his
brother Panænus, who worked in association with him.
As a sculptor, he is said to have had for his first master
in Athens Hegias, who is coupled by Lucian with
Critius and Nesiotes, the sculptors of the *Tyrannicides*,
as representing the hardness and accuracy and nervous
vigour of the early masters of athletic art. Tradition
gives, as the next master of Phidias, Ageladas of Argos,

the head of the athletic school of the Peloponnese;
whether the story be true or not—and there is no
improbability about it—it certainly represents a correct
artistic criticism.  The severity and dignity of Peloponnesian art have left their trace upon the work of
Phidias; he might, indeed, have learnt from his Attic
master the strenuous accuracy that marks the *Tyrannicides*; but hardly the quiet and unobtrusive mastery
which we see in the treatment of the nude in the
Parthenon sculptures.  The earliest period of Phidias'
artistic career of which we have any clear record is the
time of Cimon's predominance at Athens, which lasted
from about 472 B.C. to 461 B.C.  It is probably to this
time that we must attribute the series of monuments
directly commemorative of the Persian wars, and
especially of the Athenian victory of Marathon, and the
glory of Cimon's father Miltiades.  Some of these works
are expressly said to have been provided from the spoils
of Marathon, and so might at first sight appear to have
been set up immediately after the battle; for instance,
the bronze group of the *Athenian Heroes* dedicated at
Delphi; but the disgrace of Miltiades soon after his
great victory makes it improbable that a group in which
he was a prominent figure would have been set up by
the Athenians before the rehabilitation of his memory
by his son Cimon.  The group represented Athena and

Apollo, tne heroes of the ten Athenian tribes, and also
Theseus, Codrus, and Miltiades himself. Such a combination of divine, mythical, and historical persons may
seem to us lacking in simplicity and sincerity ; but it was
of a kind not unknown in Greece both earlier and later.
Had it been a group in the usual modern sense—that
is to say, had there been any common action or motive
of relation between the various figures—it would seem
even more strange. But the statues were, in all
probability, merely juxtaposed upon a common base;
and though the compliment to Miltiades, in being
dedicated in such company, was a high one, it implies
neither a claim to superhuman honours nor a purely
allegorical association with mythical persons such as
we are used to in a seventeenth-century "apotheosis."
Beyond the subject, we have no information what this
group was like; that it was held in high esteem in later
times is shown by the fact that when, in Hellenistic
times, new tribal heroes were adopted by the Athenians
from among the Macedonian and Egyptian kings, their
statues were added to this Marathonian trophy. Another
work that had direct relation to the Persian wars was
the statue of *Athena Areia* at Platæa, made from the
Platæans' share of the spoils of Marathon. This was
of gilded wood, with the face and hands and feet of
marble—a technique commonly called acrolithic, and

producing an effect similar to that of the costlier
materials of gold and ivory.  An early statue of Phidias
in this chryselephantine technique, which he was to apply
later to his most famous works, was an *Athena* at Pellene
in Achaia.  Copies of this statue are preserved on the
coins of Pellene, and show that the goddess was represented as striking with her spear in her raised right
hand, her shield on her left arm—a type common in
archaic art, and repeated, in appropriate surroundings,
in at least one of the pediments of the Parthenon, but
so unlike our preconception of the design of Phidias for
a statue of the goddess, that some doubt may occur as
to the correctness of Pausanias' attribution of the
work to Phidias.   It was, however, admittedly an early
work ; the type at Pellene may have been fixed by a
hieratic tradition too strong for the young Athenian
artist to ignore ; and, moreover, in the pose of the
statue, especially in the way in which one leg is modelled
through the drapery, while its heavy folds completely
envelop and conceal the other, we may see a well-
known Phidian characteristic. On the skirt are horizontal
bands, which may well represent rich lines of relief or
damascening, in imitation of woven designs, such as
suit both the subject and the technique.

The largest and most famous of all the early works
of Phidias was the colossal bronze *Athena,* set up in the

PLATE XX

HEAD OF ATHENA, IN JACOBSEN COLLECTION, COPENHAGEN

*To face p.* 87

open on the Acropolis at Athens; this was said to
have been provided from a tithe of the spoils of Marathon, and therefore was most probably, like the other
Marathonian trophies, set up during Cimon's predominance in Athens.[1]  This was the statue of which the
point of the spear and the crest of the helmet were
visible from the sea to those coasting along from
Sunium to the Piræus.  This statement is not only
valuable as showing the great size of the statue, but
also as indicating its pose; the spear must have been
resting upon the ground, so that its point stood out
above the head of the goddess.  The statue is represented upon the views of the Acropolis which we find
upon some Athenian coins of Roman date; it stands
out conspicuous between the Parthenon and the Propylæa; but there is no consistency in the pose of the
figure on these coins; and, even if there were, the scale
is too small to allow of any details.  On the other hand,
a figure of Athena which appears on coins has been
thought to be derived from the colossal bronze statue;
it shows the goddess standing, with both arms lowered,
her right holding the spear, of which the butt rests
upon the ground, while the point, sloping a good deal
outwards, reaches above the level of her head; on her
left arm is her shield, and her head is turned towards

[1] It is customary now to doubt this, but on no sufficient grounds.

her right shoulder.   There is in a late Byzantine
chronicle a somewhat rhetorical description of a
colossal bronze statue standing in the Forum of Con-
stantine, and destroyed in a riot in A.D. 1203; it has
been suggested that this was the identical statue made by
Phidias for the Athenian Acropolis.   If so, it is tanta-
lising to think that it should have survived so long,
and then only have been destroyed by an accident.
The later description does not in every detail agree with
earlier information about the statue; the attributes, at
least, seem to have been left behind.   But some characteristics seem to rest on direct observation, such as the
turn of the head to the right, the length and beauty of
the neck, and the hair welling out beneath the helmet.
A head in the Jacobsen collection at Copenhagen corresponds both to the description and copies of the
statue, and also to what we should expect of the earlier
work of Phidias.   The head is turned over the right
shoulder in a way that displays the beauty of the neck,
and the hair wells out beneath the helmet; the whole
is treated with a breadth and dignity that suggest a
colossal work, and a work of the fifth century; the eyes
are hollowed out in a way that suggests a bronze
original.   But although the identification is probable,
it is not certain enough to form the basis of a study of
the earlier manner of Phidias.

It is probable that other works of Phidias may
belong to the time of Cimon's predominance in Athens.
But it was the exile of Cimon and the beginning of the
predominance of Pericles in 460 B.C. that brought with
it also the era of the supreme artistic influence of
Phidias. Cimon had, indeed, prepared the Athenian
Acropolis to receive the great buildings of the Periclean
age by surrounding it with magnificent walls, and ter-
racing it so as to enlarge its area; but there is little
evidence that he set up any monuments within it except
the colossal bronze statue of the goddess. Even the
huge foundation on which the Parthenon now stands,
and which was evidently prepared for a previous temple
of slightly different plan, is now generally attributed
to an earlier date than that of Cimon. With the age
of Pericles came the transference of the treasure of the
Delian league to Athens, its transformation from a
contribution into a tribute, and its application to the
splendour of Athens by the construction of such buildings as the Parthenon and the Propylæa. All this
work, which enriched the city with incomparable
masterpieces of architecture and sculpture, was, as we
are expressly told, under the direction of Phidias, who,
out of his friendship for Pericles, gave his supervision
to the whole, many distinguished architects and other
artists assisting him. It is somewhat difficult, in these

circumstances, to estimate exactly how much is to be attributed individually to Phidias. No one, for example, would deny Ictinus the credit of designing the Parthenon, or Mnesicles of designing the Propylæa, though both buildings formed part of a general scheme laid out by Pericles in consultation with Phidias. In the case of sculpture, however, we have already noticed that there is every reason to believe that Phidias exercised a more direct supervision and was more immediately responsible, at least for the design. But the only part of the work which is directly attributed to him by ancient authorities is the colossal gold and ivory statue of *Athena Parthenos* in the cella of the Parthenon—a statue which ranked with the *Zeus* at Olympia as the most characteristic work of Phidias. This statue has, of course, completely disappeared; all that can now be seen upon the site are the traces of the pedestal upon which it stood. We possess, however, a good many more or less direct copies from the statue, though it unfortunately happens that their artistic merit is almost exactly in inverse proportion to their fidelity to the original from which they are derived. They do not really give us much information beyond what we can derive from the description of the statue by Pausanias and from our general knowledge of the sculpture of the time. They serve, however, as a help in an endeavour

PLATE XXI

SMALL COPY OF ATHENA PARTHENOS, IN MADRID

*To face p. 90*

to imagine what the original must have been like, even
if they preserve us very little of its artistic character.

The goddess was represented standing, a figure of
Victory on her extended right hand, her left hand resting upon her shield, and also holding her spear; within
the hollow of her shield was coiled the sacred serpent.
She was clothed in a simple Doric chiton, of which the
upper fold fell below her waist and was confined by a
girdle, meeting in front in a snaky clasp; her weight
rested mainly on her right leg, in front of which the
dress fell in heavy and rigid folds; her left leg was
bent, and so, as the knee projected forward, was
modelled through the drapery—a common device in
the sculpture of the period. Every available part of
the statue and its accessories was covered with the
richest decoration. The description of Pausanias would
of itself suffice to show this. " On the middle of her
helmet," he says, " is set a Sphinx, and gryphons on
either side of it; on her breast is wrought a head of
Medusa. . . . And on the basis of the statue is represented the birth of Pandora." We may supplement
this from Pliny : " On the convex surface of her shield
was embossed the battle of the Amazons, on its concave
side was the fight of the Gods and the Giants ; on her
sandals were the Lapithæ and Centaurs ; Phidias indeed
regarded every available field as suited to the exercise

of his art." It was hardly to be expected that any small copy of a colossal statue would preserve for us all this ornamentation. But, with the exception of the relief on the margin of the sandals—which can be paralleled elsewhere—we find all of it indicated on one or another of the copies we possess, sufficiently at least for us to judge of its position, and, to some extent, of its decorative effect; while some copies show us even more details of decoration not mentioned by the literary authorities, such as a row of the fore-parts of horses, projecting from the frontlet of the helmet above the forehead of the goddess. In some cases, again, we find an inconsistency between the descriptions and the copies; thus the animals supporting the two lateral crests, described by Pausanias as gryphons, appear in several copies as winged horses. A coincidence in mistake between these copies is hardly probable; and therefore it seems more probable that Pausanias was mistaken; the fact that he adds a disquisition about the gryphons does not really add to the weight of his evidence; for this was evidently added in his study at home, while the mention of the gryphons must be taken either from his notes made on the spot or from an authority from which he borrowed.

Such discrepancies, however, only affect matters of detail; it is their general correspondence in pose,

attributes, and decoration that has led to the identification of various copies as directly derived from the
great chryselephantine statue of Phidias. Apart from
such correspondence, it would by no means have been
necessary to assume that any extant statues of *Athena*
were directly copied from the colossal figure in the
Parthenon. It was not, indeed, a common thing for
such colossal statues to be copied upon a smaller scale;
and we do not, perhaps, possess any other certain
example of a life-size copy of a colossal work. In this
case, however, the evidence is convincing; we have, in
the first place, coins both of Athens and of other
cities which reproduce the *Athena Parthenos;* then
there are reliefs that are evidently intended to represent not merely *Athena* but the *Athena˘ Parthenos,*
in various connections. Complete copies have been
recognised in three statuettes; one, known as the
Lenormant statuette, is an unfinished sketch, but useful
for its indication of figures on the basis and on the
outside of the shield; another, known, from the place
where it was found in modern Athens, as the Varvakeion
statuette, is complete and in good preservation, and
therefore is useful as showing the position of various
accessories, though it omits the reliefs upon the shield;
but it is a base and mechanical piece of work, and
shows no feeling for the grandeur of its original. The

third statuette was recently discovered at Patras; it is headless and armless, but is valuable as preserving a portion of the shield with its reliefs. In addition to these statuettes there are several statues—notably one in Madrid, about half life-size, and another in Paris— which are evidently meant to reproduce the *Athena Parthenos*, and there are two or three heads also which seem to show some attempt to imitate in marble the surface and colouring of the chryselephantine work— one in Berlin, another found in the Odeum of Herodes at Athens. All these, however, can do little but show us the nature of the attributes and drapery, the pose of the statue, and the physical type of the face— matters on which, allowing for their difference of workmanship, they are fairly in agreement. The character of the statue itself we must infer from other sources. These are partly to be found in the surviving sculptures from the Parthenon, partly in other statues which preserve the Phidian tradition, and which must be considered later.

A complete description of the sculpture that decorated the Parthenon cannot be given here; but in an attempt to estimate the artistic qualities of Phidias, it is impossible to pass over the extant sculptures that stand in the closest relation to him. The vast . ount of this sculpture—ninety-two metopes, about fift· colossal

figures in the pediments, and over 520 feet of continuous frieze—precludes the possibility that one man
could have even designed the whole in detail, much less
executed it in marble. On the other hand, a great deal
of the sculpture differs so greatly from what we find in
Athens at a slightly earlier date that we seem justified
in recognising in it the stamp of a great and original
genius; and there is no artist but Phidias himself to
whom so marvellous an advance can with any probability be assigned. In this matter, however, we may
make a distinction between the different parts of the
sculptures. The metopes which stood over the outer
colonnade must have been placed in position at an
early stage in the building; and their separation into
a series of isolated groups made it easy to distribute
them among different artists, subject only to a general
scheme of decoration. Those which survive show clear
traces of such a distribution. Most of them come from
the south side of the building, and represent combats
of Lapithæ and Centaurs; those from the other sides are
for the most part too much damaged to afford any clear
indications of style. Even the Centaur metopes, for all
their similarity of subject, show the most astonishing
diversity of artistic character. Some—especially of
those which contain female figures—have the stiff and
awkward execution of archaic art; many others show an

exaggerated angularity of action, and a delight in the
tricks of the wrestling school, which harmonise well
with the dry treatment of the surface and over-emphasis
of the muscles and which betray the work of a school
trained in athletic subjects. We know that such a
school existed in Athens in the earlier part of the fifth
century; and it was natural enough that it should
take its share in the new activity under Pericles,
before Phidias had yet gathered around him a group
of sculptors trained in his own methods and imbued
with his spirit. So far as the work of Phidias himself
is concerned, these earlier metopes may be ignored;
but there are others which show the same qualities
which we admire in the pediments and in the best
parts of the frieze—a majestic conception of the
human figure, a modelling true to nature and free
from all exaggeration, a masterly composition, and
perfect adaptation of the design to the space. Above
all, the harmonious impression conveyed by the whole,
the avoidance alike of the conventional and the accidental, are found in these finest metopes as in the
rest of the sculptures of the Parthenon, and seem to
carry the peculiar stamp of the genius of Phidias.
This genius finds, however, fuller expression in the
pediments. We have, indeed, only a few figures from
the pediments left—and those for the most part sub-

ordinate ones. As to the composition as a whole, and its artistic effect, these figures can give us little information. In the case of the eastern pediment, which represented the birth of Athena, a careful archæological study of all extant data has led to various reconstructions of the whole group which probably, viewed as mere diagrams, give a fairly correct notion of its arrangement; but the complete restorations that have been based on them only suffice to show the impossibility of recovering anything like the artistic effect of the original. In the case of the western pediment we have a more satisfactory record in the drawings attributed to Carrey, made in 1674, when the group was still fairly complete. Of course it is impossible for a slight sketch such as his to convey any adequate impression of the great group; but it does at least indicate the general lines of the composition. We can see from it, for example, the relation of the two principal figures of *Posidon and Athena,* who had met in rivalry to claim the land of Attica. Each is in vigorous motion away from the centre, their paths apparently crossing each other, and each half turned back towards the opponent. Thus we have an appearance of cross-strain which is most effective as the centre of a great architectural composition, and which we find also in one of the finest of the Centaur metopes. But it is, above all, to the

G

extant figures that we must turn if we wish to appreciate the character of the sculptures of the Parthenon.
We have still left, in the British Museum, in addition
to the figures of the rising sun and the setting moon
that framed the whole, the three extreme figures of the
group at each side; and thus it is possible, so far as this
part of the work is concerned, to judge even of the
composition.  The subtle and varied symmetry with
which the two sets of three figures balance each other
has often been pointed out.  But it is, above all, the
sculptured forms of the extant figures that place their
author immeasurably above his predecessors, and cause
him to be recognised by all artists as attaining a perfection in sculpture such as has never been surpassed in
any other age.  His treatment of the nude male figure,
as it may be seen in the *Theseus* and the *Ilissus*,
contrasts alike with the muscular emphasis of Myron's
work and with the formal perfection of Polyclitus;
both figures have individuality and character, the one
in his monumental repose, the other in the delicacy and
almost fluid quality of his flesh, which goes far to
confirm his usual identification as a river-god.  But
perhaps, for their contrast with the work of a slightly
earlier date in Athens, the draped figures, such as the
*Three Fates* or the *Demeter and Persephone*, are even
more wonderful.  The earlier Attic sculptors had,

PLATE XXII

IRIS, DEMETER, AND PERSEPHONE, FROM THE E. PEDIMENT OF THE PARTHENON

*To face p. 98*

indeed, given great pains to the study of drapery; but the result was the elaboration of a stiff and formal system of folds rather than an approximation to the natural effect. Here in these pedimental figures we find the most wonderful richness and variety, and the most perfect truth to nature. But there is also an individuality of style so marked that it is easy for any one who has made a study of the sculptures of the Parthenon to pick out portions of them from a heap of miscellaneous fragments. It is impossible to express this character in words; but one may notice certain qualities which at least contribute to it. Of these perhaps the chief is harmony—the harmonious relation of every part to the whole, of the drapery to the human form, of every minute fold to the general scheme of arrangement, the absence of anything accidental to mar the complete satisfaction and repose with which the eye can travel over the whole surface of the marble. Closely associated with this harmony is the complete absence of exaggeration or of striving after effect. The forms of the body are revealed or suggested by the drapery which covers them; but in a way that is not at all inconsistent with the material and texture of the drapery itself, whether thicker or thinner. The stuff never clings, as if damp, to the limbs of the figures, nor is it ever contorted into tempestuous or disordered folds. The

whole of it is separated into masses of broad and
flowing composition; and each of these masses is sub-
divided into minor folds, and even the surface of each of
these folds is worked in careful relation to its texture;
yet with all this elaboration there is nothing laboured.
Later Greek artists, not to speak of more modern imitators, who have been influenced by this wonderful
treatment of drapery, have almost always fallen into
one extreme or the other; either its breadth and simplicity has led them to an undue severity, and even,
sometimes, to a dry mannerism; or else its richness
and sense of texture has induced them to adopt those
devices of clinging, sweeping, or contorted folds of which
we notice the absence in the Parthenon pediments.
It is most fortunate that chance should have preserved
for us these figures, which enable us to see what Greek
work was like in Attic originals of the greatest period;
without them, we could never have inferred their finer
qualities from any copies or imitations. The draped
figures from the Parthenon pediments show the same
breadth and majesty of type that we may see in the
nude male figures. The horses' heads, too, show similar
characteristics, both those of the Sun, flung up to catch
the breath of morning, or those of the Moon; for mere
sense of texture nothing can rival the head now in the
British Museum from the extreme end of the east

PLATE XXIII

FIGURE FROM W. PEDIMENT OF PARTHENON

*To face p.* 100

pediment. The soft, quivering skin around the nostril is so delicately rendered that it is difficult to realise, as we look at it, that it is marble and not living flesh; yet here again the effect is gained with the utmost direct- ness and simplicity. It is, in fact, difficult not to believe that some, at least, of the sculpture of the pediments must have been executed as well as designed by the hand of the master; if not, it would be even more wonderful that he should have been able to inspire his assistants with a skill and sureness of work so worthy of the design.

The frieze of the Parthenon has much in common with the pediments, but it is far more uneven in the quality of its execution. For its position on the temple, for the choice of a processional subject, admirably suited to be seen between the columns as one walks along outside the building, and even for the low relief, slightly higher at the top than at the bottom, and thereby suited to the lighting from below in its avoiding of heavy shadows, the architect Ictinus may be held directly responsible, though doubtless in con- sultation with Phidias. And in the selection of the Pan-Athenaic festival as a theme which gave scope for the representation of all that was most characteristic of Attic life in the service of the goddess—the magistrates and other officials, the noble maidens, the colonists, the resident foreigners, the sacrificial animals

the chariots and the knightly cavalry—we may recognise the political designs of Pericles himself. But the
composition of the frieze, the relation and distribution
of its various parts, the arrangement of its groups and
figures, show clearly a common design which we must
attribute to a single master, and this master can hardly
be any other than Phidias, to whom we must probably
assign at least a preliminary sketch of the whole. But
it was the custom, as we may infer from inscriptions, to
allow a good deal of initiative to the individual assistants
who undertook different figures or groups in such a
composition as this ; and a careful study of the work in
detail, if it does not enable us to distinguish all the
hands employed, and to assign to each his portion of
the whole, at least allows us to pick out certain pieces
of the work as showing the same characteristics, and so
almost certainly to be attributed to the same sculptor.
There is, indeed, a certain uniformity of style throughout which shows that Phidias had by this time trained
a staff of assistants fit to carry out his designs; but
some of them do this with a vigour of touch, a certainty
and boldness of work worthy of the master himself,
while others show a somewhat dry and mechanical
method of attaining the prescribed result. As an
example of the latter, we may take the slab with the
three deities—Posidon, Apollo, and a goddess—which

PLATE XXIV

CHARIOT HORSES, FROM S. FRIEZE OF PARTHENON

*To face p.* 163

is one of the best preserved pieces of the whole. An
instance of the more spontaneous work is to be seen in
the heads of the chariot-horses reproduced in Pl. XXV.
It is of this piece that Mr. Ruskin wrote, in his
" Aratra Pentelici ": " The projection of the four
horses, one behind the other, is certainly not more,
altogether, than three-quarters of an inch from the flat
ground, and the one in front does not in reality project
more than the one behind it, yet, by mere drawing, you
see the sculptor has got them to appear to recede in due
order, and by the soft rounding of the flesh surfaces, and
modulation of the veins, he has taken away all look of
flatness from the necks. He has drawn the eyes and
nostrils with dark incision, careful as the finest touches
of a painter's pencil ; and then, at last, when he comes
to the manes, he has let fly hand and chisel with their
full force ; and where a base workman (above all, if he
had modelled the thing in clay first) would have lost
himself in laborious imitation of hair, the Greek has
struck the tresses out with angular incisions, deep
driven, every one in appointed place and deliberate
curve, yet flowing so free under his noble hand that you
cannot alter, without harm, the bending of any single
ridge, nor contract, nor extend, a point of them." Here,
as Ruskin says, " you may recognise the decision of "
the sculptor's " thought and glow of his temper, no less

in the workmanship than the design." It is a tempting
inference to refer the execution of the few bits of
the frieze that are on this level of excellence to Phidias
himself, and to suggest that he may have done them as
an example to the assistants who were to carry out the
rest; if this were not the case, it is all the more
remarkable to find such qualities in the work of a
subordinate, and it makes us realise that Phidias had
the power of inspiring his pupils and assistants to
produce work hardly to be distinguished from his own
—a fact attested in the case of certain well-known
statues, and so, perhaps, the less surprising in architectural sculpture such as this. In any case, the characteristics are similar to those we noticed in the draped
figures of the pediments; we see the same harmony,
the same subordination of every minute touch to the
general effect, and also the same breadth combined
with delicacy in the modelling. In the less successful
portions of the frieze, either breadth or delicacy tends
to be in some degree lost, as we might expect would be
the case in the work of subordinates who were unable
to attain the high standard set them by the master.
An example of variety may be seen if we compare the
horses' heads just mentioned with the horses, for instance, of the two riders from the west frieze (Pl. XXV.).
Here, too, the execution is full of life and spirit; but

PLATE XXV

To face p. 104

ATHENIAN KNIGHTS, FROM W. FRIEZE OF PARTHENON

PLATE XXVI

To face p. 105

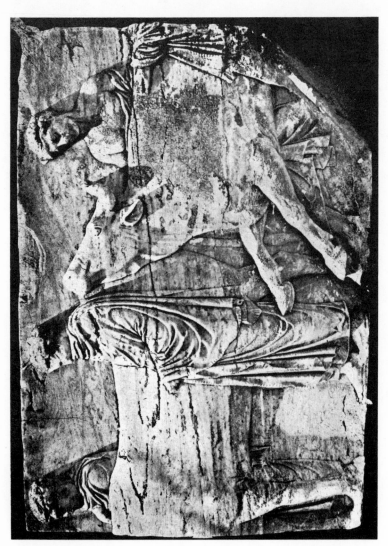

YOUTHS WITH COWS, FROM N. FRIEZE OF PARTHENON

the treatment of the eyes and manes of the horses is totally different, and the whole modelling is of another character. The slab with the cows (Pl. XXVI.) shows a very beautiful and restrained treatment of drapery, perhaps as simple and effective as anything in the Parthenon sculptures. It is evidently very difficult for us to say exactly how much of all this work is to be attributed to Phidias individually; but we may, without hesitation, assign to his direct influence and teaching the fact that a body of sculptors could be found capable of producing in a short time all this mass of sculpture on the Parthenon—sculpture which, in its character, can easily be distinguished not only from earlier work, but even from contemporary work elsewhere and from later imitations.

It is probable that during his activity on the Parthenon and his general direction of work at Athens, Phidias also produced some other statues; but the second great undertaking with which his name was associated by the Greeks was the making of the colossal gold and ivory statue of *Zeus* at Olympia. We have, indeed, more literary information about this statue than about any other work of his, including many rhetorical appreciations and a long and detailed description by Pausanias; but we would gladly exchange all of these for a little more knowledge of the statue itself, apart from details or accessories, or for a little more trustworthy information as to the time when it was made and the conditions under which it was prepared. It is even a matter of dispute whether Phidias worked at Olympia before he went to help Pericles to beautify Athens, or went to Olympia after his disgrace and exile from Athens. This disgrace was a purely political matter, a part of the attack on Pericles in the days of his waning influence. Phidias was first charged with embezzlement of the gold supplied to him for the great statue ; and when he was able to refute this accusation by weighing it, a new charge was brought against him of sacrilege, in placing his own portrait and that of Pericles on the shield of the goddess. We have already noticed this portrait of a vigorous old man with bald head as our only evidence for the age of the artist. He appears to have been condemned ; but if, as appears likely, he was afterwards employed at Olympia, it seems that the Greeks generally did not take the matter seriously. At Olympia the conditions were not the same as at Athens. The great temple in which the statue was to be set up was already built, and its sculptures, impressive but uncouth in execution as compared with those of the Parthenon, were in their places on the building. All that could be done to give a fitting architectural frame to the colossal statue consisted of certain modifications and additions in the cella, in which Phidias was helped by his brother, the painter Panænus, and other collaborators. He seems to have been given every facility, and provided with a studio the same size as the cella of the temple; this studio was shown to visitors even down to the time of Pausanias as a memorial of the master. The statue, being seated, was even more colossal in size than the *Athena Parthenos*, and it is noted that the god could not have arisen from his throne without putting his head through the roof—a proportion between temple and statue that would hardly have been chosen if, as at Athens, both had been part of a great and uniform design. Copies on coins suffice to show the position of the god, who was seated upright, with his head slightly bent forward; his cloak, falling over his left shoulder and across his knees, left the upper part of his body bare, his right hand held a figure of Victory, his left rested on a long sceptre surmounted by an eagle; the whole effect is of simple dignity, in contrast with the somewhat theatrical attitude which we find in some later statues. The description of Pausanias gives us an excellent notion of the rich accessories. The throne was supported by figures of Victory, and on its seat and cross-bars were series of figures representing such subjects as the slaying of the children of Niobe and the battle of Heracles and the Amazons; and there were groups of the *Graces* and the *Seasons* surmounting the back of the throne. There were screens between the supports, which were ornamented with paintings at the sides and back, but in front were left plain blue, so as to show up the figure. The golden garments of the god, too, were damascened with figures of animals and lily flowers; and the whole, both throne and statue, was a variegated mass of ivory and ebony, of gold and precious stones. The richness of this decoration was well suited to the subdued and reflected light which came through the great door or filtered through the marble roof of the temple. The expression of the face shows the same calm dignity and simplicity of style which distinguishes the whole statue; of this we can judge partly from reproductions on Roman coins, partly from a head now in Boston, which we can, by the help of these coins, identify as far nearer to the Phidian type than the imposing but somewhat theatrical heads of *Zeus* produced by later Greek art, for example, the *Zeus of Otricoli*. In the Boston head, as on the coins, the hair and beard are treated in smoothly waved tresses, in contrast to the mane-like and dishevelled locks of later art; the eyes are not deeply set in the head, nor is the brow so broad and massive. It is possible that in this Boston head we may see certain

PLATE XXVII

HEAD OF ZEUS, IN BOSTON

*To face p.* 108

qualities that have been introduced by a copyist under
the influence of fourth-century art; there is a certain
softness of modelling and lack of the breadth and
majesty of design which we can recognise in the coin;
in this last respect, indeed, the Otricoli head may even
preserve for us more of the Phidian character. But if
the Otricoli head is inspired with something of the
majesty of the Olympian god, and if the Boston head
preserves for us much of the general appearance of the
masterpiece of Phidias, we must admit that both alike
fail to give us, by themselves, any complete notion of
the original. For this we are, after all, reduced to the
descriptions of ancient writers. Such descriptions, as
Lessing pointed out, are of little use when they try to
describe a work of art in detail; the only way in which
a literary description can really help us is when it
describes the effect produced by such a work upon those
who see it. We have such testimony from many
ancient writers; and although some of them are in-
fected by the rhetorical strain of their time, they seem
to express something like the common feeling of cultured
Greeks about the matter. Thus we are told that " the
beauty of this statue actually contributed an addition
to the received religion; so adequate to the majesty of
the god was the grandeur of the work," or that those
who had seen it could not easily imagine the god in any

other form.  The most striking passage of all is, perhaps, the one in which Dio Chrysostom says, " any man who is heavy-laden in soul, who has suffered many misfortunes and sorrows in his life, and who has no comfort of sweet sleep, even such a one, I think, if he stood opposite this statue, would forget all the dangers and hardships of this mortal life."  Such an ideal creation, the mere contemplation of which could take a man out of himself, and elevate him to a region of imagination outside the petty worries and accidents that surrounded him, was of great importance not only to the history of art but to that of religion also.   But we must guard against the impression that the *Zeus* of Phidias was a mere philosophical abstraction, a monotheistic impersonation of the supreme deity.   Phidias himself stated that the Homeric conception of Zeus was in his mind; and his statue was regarded as the guardian and saviour of Hellas, and of a Hellas united and harmonious as her wisest citizens sometimes dreamed of her.  If no copy and no description is adequate to convey to us an impression of the statue, we must be content to realise its character, in part at least, from the influence of the master, as it can be traced in the statues of the gods made by his contemporaries and immediate successors, with their new expression of a majesty and divinity such as earlier sculptors had been unable to render,

PLATE XXVIII

"LEMNIAN ATHENA"; STATUE IN DRESDEN,
WITH BOLOGNA HEAD ADDED

*To face p.* 111

while later art, however skilful, never attains to the same nobility in its ideals.

Several other statues of the gods are recorded as due to the hand of Phidias, in addition to the colossal ones we have just noticed; and among them the pre-eminent place is assigned, by critics so widely different as Pausanias and Lucian, to the statue known as the *Lemnian Athena*, which Lucian even goes so far as to call the most beautiful of the works of Phidias. The goddess was especially worshipped in the island of Lemnos in association with Posidon. Pausanias tells us that the statue was so called from those who dedicated it; that is to say, in all probability, the Athenian colonists who settled in Lemnos about 450 B.C., and who dedicated to their goddess in her own city her image as she was worshipped in Lemnos. The statue was probably in bronze, and it has been inferred, on somewhat doubtful evidence, that she was bare-headed. In view of the enthusiasm of so competent a critic as Lucian, the identification of this *Lemnian Athena* in two or three copies, and above all in a beautiful head at Bologna which Furtwängler, with great acumen, recognised as belonging to a type of *Athena* represented by two statues at Dresden, aroused the greatest interest; and although there have been some dissentient or sceptical voices, the great majority of

archæologists have accepted the identification as
proved. Where the external evidence is so scanty, the
ultimate appeal must be to the evidence of style.
There can be no doubt that the Bologna head is derived
from a bronze original, and the *Lemnian Athena* was
probably of bronze ; and the two statues at Dresden
show the simple and dignified arrangement of drapery,
falling on one side in heavy columnar folds, and on the
other modelling the form of the knee, which we see
in the *Athena Parthenos*, and which we may recognise
also in other works, such as the *Caryatids* of the Erech-
theum, that show strong Phidian influence. The type
of the draped figure clearly belongs to his period and
school. The head, indeed, does not resemble those we
find in the Parthenon sculptures, nor those of the copies
of the *Athena Parthenos*. But, it may be answered,
neither architectural sculptures nor late copies of a
colossal chryselephantine work can supply us with adequate criteria for judging what a life-size bronze statue
by Phidias would be like. In that case, however, we are
reduced to inferences and probabilities ; and though
the result may meet with general acceptance, it is
impossible to deny the right of scepticism to those
whose study of the art of Phidias has led them to a
different conclusion. It is to be remembered that
before Furtwängler's identification the Bologna head was

PLATE XXIX

"LEMNIAN ATHENA"; HEAD IN BOLOGNA

*To face* **p.** 112

generally regarded as Polyclitan rather than Attic ; and
although the action and reaction on each other of the
Peloponnesian and Attic schools in the fifth century were
very strong, as we shall see in the case of Polyclitus,
this fact must be allowed its weight in the discussion.

The Bologna head certainly belonged to a statue of
*Athena.* Whether this statue was by Phidias or made
under strong Phidian influence, it shows a more personal
and individual presentation of the goddess than we
find in the colossal statues ; the bare-headed type of
*Athena,* carrying her helmet in her hand, was a
favourite one in fifth-century art. We need not
wonder that such a type appealed by its beauty to
later critics, especially when they were accustomed to
the more individualistic work of the fourth century.
Here we have a statue of *Athena,* which does not lose
anything of the majesty and dignity of the goddess,
while it divests her of her more formidable attributes and
of her more abstract ideal of divinity. When we consider the marvellous advance that Phidias made beyond
his predecessors in other respects, we certainly cannot
assert with confidence that he may not, in this statue,
have also anticipated something of what was best and
most interesting in the rendering of the gods by those
who followed him. If the identification of his *Lemnian
Athena* be accepted, we shall see in his work a versatility

H

and a charm which may possibly attract some modern
admirers even more than the unrivalled qualities of
the Elgin marbles. Lucian especially selects from the
*Lemnia* the outline of the whole face, the delicacy of
the cheeks, and the symmetry of the nose. There is no
difficulty in recognising these excellences in the Bologna
head; to them we may add the way in which the hair
wells out from beneath the band and overshadows
the brow. We may see very much the same effect in
the beautiful head of the *Farnese Hera* which, though
probably Polyclitan in character, shows the same
combination of severity and delicacy which is conspicuous in the Bologna head.

Of another bronze statue by Phidias on the Athenian
Acropolis, *Apollo of the Locusts*, we know nothing but
the name; his *Aphrodite Urania* was probably inspired
by the same distinction between heavenly and earthly
love which we find in Plato and later poets, and which
was a curious inversion of mythological fact. He made
another statue of this same goddess for Elis, probably during his employment at Olympia. Of his *Amazon*, made
for Ephesus, we shall have to speak under Polyclitus.
Among other extant statues that have been associated
with Phidias, none is better worth mention here than
the marble statue of *Apollo* found in the Tiber, and
now exhibited in the Museo delle Terme at Rome. This

PLATE XXX

APOLLO, IN THE MUSEO DELLE TERME
AT ROME

*To face p.* 114

PLATE XXXI

HEAD OF APOLLO, IN THE MUSEO DELLE TERME AT ROME

*To face p.* 115

shows a charming figure of the youthful god, in pose
and proportions very like the figures from the Parthenon frieze. The hair and face also, allowing for their
more careful execution, show the same affinities. The
type is a more advanced example of that we see in the
Choiseul Gouffier *Apollo* and the *Iacchus* of the British
Museum, but lighter and more graceful. It has been
suggested that we should see here an early work of
Phidias; and it may well represent the stage that had
been reached by Attic sculpture at the beginning of its
new inspiration under its greatest master.

It is interesting to compare with this the reflection of
the same influence on a piece of sculpture found far
away from Athens, the so-called *Lycian Sarcophagus*
from Sidon. Here we have a work made for an eastern
prince by a Greek artist who probably was one of those
who worked with Phidias upon the Parthenon, and who
has caught both the spirit of the design and the perfection of technique which we see in the Elgin marbles.
On one side of the *Sarcophagus* is a group of horsemen
employed in a boar hunt, who remind us irresistibly, in
the ease of their bearing and the grace and variety of
the design, of the Athenian knights on the Parthenon
frieze; on the other are Amazons in chariots at a lion
hunt, and the heads of these figures, reproduced here,
give perhaps as beautiful an example as we possess of

the Phidian type of head, with its regular and simply modelled features; the richly waved hair, soft in texture, yet with no accidental disorder to distract us from the harmony of the whole design, is also comparable to that of the most careful work in the frieze. The discovery of such sculpture as this at Sidon shows us how far the influence of Attic art under Phidias had spread. In Greece itself, the artists who had worked with him again diffused the tradition whereby Athens seemed to have drawn to itself and to have glorified, in the sculpture made in the time of Pericles and Phidias, all that was best and most characteristic in the attainments of the earlier schools of Hellas.

PLATE XXXII

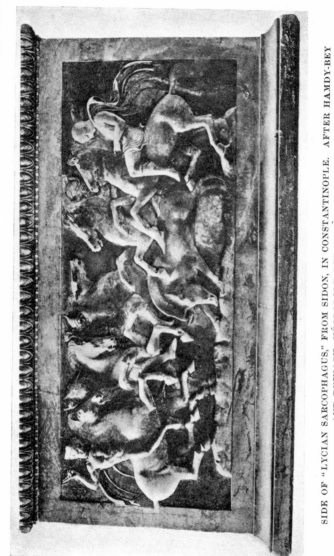

To face p. 116

SIDE OF "LYCIAN SARCOPHAGUS," FROM SIDON, IN CONSTANTINOPLE. AFTER HAMDY-BEY
AND REINACH, *NÉCROPOLE ROYALE À SIDON*, PL. XVI

PLATE XXXIII

HEADS FROM "LYCIAN SARCOPHAGUS." AFTER HAMDY-BEY AND
REINACH, *OP. CIT.*, DETAIL ON PL. XIV

*Between pp.* 116 *and* 117

# CHAPTER V

## POLYCLITUS

POLYCLITUS is the most typical of all Greek sculptors; and perhaps, for this very reason, his personality may seem at first sight less interesting than that of others whose work was less perfect. When we read the ancient criticisms of his style, we are often more impressed by the statement that his statues were almost all of a uniform type, that he affected with monotony certain poses and proportions, than by the estimate which ranks him even above Phidias as the most consummate master of sculpture. Even if we make some allowance for the fact that this last appreciation was the product of a school of criticism which set itself especially to extol the Argive and Sicyonian schools of sculpture, we must remember that it represents the view of many of those best acquainted with Greek art. We have already noticed how the very limitation of early Greek sculpture contributed in no small degree to its rapid and certain advance. The athletic statues

made by Polyclitus really form the culmination of a
series which begins with the early *Apollo* statues,
the ordinary nude male type of Greek sculpture in
its primitive stage.  And great as was his technical
superiority to those who made these early statues, his
'aim was not essentially different from theirs.  He did not
aim at originality or especial appropriateness of composition or pose; he accepted these as laid down by
custom or convention, or, at most, he tried to introduce
into them some slight modification or improvement.
Apart from this, he concentrated his efforts on the
highest perfection of bodily type and proportions, and
on consummate skill in technical execution in bronze.
Two sayings of his are quoted, which throw much light
on the character of his art.  One is that " Successful
attainment in art is the result of minute accuracy in a
multitude of arithmetical proportions." [1]  We must
remember that a study of theoretical proportion of
parts to one another and to the whole figure has often
been attractive to artists.  The canon adopted by the
Egyptians was, as we have seen, in all probability
borrowed entire by some of the early Greek sculptors ;
but few if any of them were content to adhere to it
with mechanical precision.  We can, as a matter of fact,
trace in many archaic statues clearly marked schemes

[1] τὸ γὰρ εὖ παρὰ μικρὸν διὰ πολλῶν ἀριθμῶν ἔφη γίνεσθαι.

of proportion ; [1] it is impossible here to follow them in
detail; but it may suffice to notice that most of the
earlier sculptors divide the face vertically in varying
proportions, the divisions usually falling at the eye, the
tip of the nose, and the mouth. In the canon of Polyclitus, on the other hand, the brow is taken as the most
essential division, a system at once more artistic and
more scientific, since it substitutes for more or less
accidental points a structural line depending on the
conformation of the skull. Again, the head is made
one-seventh of the total height, and all other details
are worked out with a similar accuracy. So systematic
a method may seem likely to lead to lifeless and
mechanical results, as in later Egyptian art ; but extant
copies of the works of Polyclitus, and the estimate in
which he was held by the Greeks, show that this was
not the case. His excellence was in great measure due
to his minute observation of nature in detail and his
careful finish of the surface, as is attested by another
characteristic saying : " The work is most difficult when
the clay comes to the nail." [2] The exact meaning of
this expression is disputable ; but it must imply that it
is the last finishing of the surface that taxes the highest

---

1 *See* Kalkmann, " Proportionen des Gesichts," 53rd Berlin Winc-
kelmannsprogramm.

2 χαλεπώτατον τὸ ἔργον. ὅταν ἐν ὄνυχι ὁ πηλὸς γένηται.

powers of the artist; and it shows that accuracy of finish as well as exact calculation of proportion was characteristic of the art of Polyclitus.

We are informed that Polyclitus not only published his theory of sculpture in a work called " The Canon," but also that, " having taught in that treatise all the proportions of the body, he carried his theory into practice by constructing a statue according to the prescriptions in the treatise, and by calling this statue, as well as the treatise, *The Canon*." There are in our museums several statues which have been identified as copies of this *Canon*; these we must consider when we come to discuss the extant works that can be attributed to Polyclitus. Before this we must take a brief survey of what is known as to his life and connections.

Polyclitus belonged to a generation somewhat younger than that of Phidias. He was employed in making statues of athletic victors before the middle of the fifth century [1]; his colossal gold and ivory statue of *Hera* in the Heræum at Argos was not begun until after the destruction of the earlier temple by fire in 423 B.C. The great dedicatory group set up after the battle of Ægospotami in 405 B.C. was made by his pupils, and he himself made a statue of *Aphrodite*

1 Of the victors he commemorated, Cyniscus won in 460 B.C., and Pythocles and Aristion in 452 B.C.

set up on the same occasion at Amyclæ. From these
dates we can infer that the period of his artistic
activity must have been much prolonged. He was
probably born during the age of the Persian Wars; and
his pupilage would fall before 460 B.C. The tradition
that Myron, Phidias, and Polyclitus were all pupils of
Ageladas of Argos has already been quoted. It is
chronologically probable in the case of the two earlier
masters. This probability, and even possibility, has
been denied in the case of Polyclitus; but the early
date which must now be assigned to some of his athletic
statues makes his career overlap that of Ageladas.
The appropriateness of assigning him as a master the
sculptor whom he was to succeed as the leader of
the great athletic school of Argive art is obvious; it
cannot be doubted that his study of athletic proportions and his skill in the working of bronze were
directly inherited from the school in which Ageladas
was his most famous predecessor. Apart from this one
tradition, we know nothing of his life except what we
can gather from his works. He probably lived entirely
at Argos, which, for the most part, held aloof from the
Peloponnesian War, and so had more leisure to cultivate
the arts of peace; though it was by no means exempt
from internal factions, one of which, in 418 B.C., led to
a massacre. In propitiation for this Polyclitus made

a statue of *Zeus Meilichios, the Merciful.*  But the most
famous of his public commissions was the *Hera* in the
Heræum, which was extolled by some as even more
beautiful than the *Zeus* of Olympia, and vindicates for
Polyclitus a fame as a maker of gods as well as of
athletes.  His figures of gods, so far as they can be dated,
seem to belong to his later years.  His earlier works
seem to have been mainly athletes, with the exception of
the *Amazon,* which he is said to have made for Ephesus
in competition with Phidias, Cresilas, and Phradmon.

Of his statue called *The Canon* we possess in our
museums several copies ; the best of them was found at
Pompeii, and is now at Naples.  It represents a young
athlete advancing at a walking pace, his right foot
planted firmly in front, and supporting the whole
weight of the body, while the left trails behind, only
the toes resting on the ground.  In his left hand he
carries a spear sloped over his left shoulder, and for
this reason was often called the *Doryphorus* or spear-
bearer.  His head is turned towards the side on which
the foot is advanced, thus emphasising the monotony
which the critics mention.  A later sculptor would almost
certainly have aimed at variety by turning the head the
other way.  The extant copies of the *Doryphorus* are
all of Roman date, and mostly in marble.  We cannot,
therefore, look to them for those refinements of bronze

PLATE XXXIV

DORYPHORUS, AFTER POLYCLITUS, AT NAPLES

*To face p.* 122

technique for which Polyclitus was especially famous.
On the other hand, they agree with one another in
their style and proportions, and so may serve as trustworthy evidence as to their original; they even preserve
in the marble many characteristics borrowed from
bronze, and one of them, the head from Herculaneum
now in Naples, is itself in bronze. All, however, are
more or less mechanical copies, and cannot give us an
adequate notion of the beauty of the work of Polyclitus. The proportions of the figure are somewhat
heavy, especially when compared with Attic work; the
muscular structure is very clearly mapped out, mostly
in broad surfaces with clear lines of demarcation between
them. The head also is very square and massive in
build, with little expression beyond that of passive
physical existence; the hair clings close to the scalp,
and is rendered in a series of little wavy curls. It is
evident that the sculptor's aim is neither interest of
subject nor of expression, but perfection of bodily form
and proportion. This he has attained to a wonderful
degree.

The satisfying effect produced on the eye by the
*Doryphorus* is probably in the main due to the same
unconscious appreciation of a subtle system of proportion that we feel also in looking at a Doric temple of
the fifth century. Though we may not know it, we

probably are constantly seeking to realise the proportion of different parts of a figure or a building to one another. When these proportions are accidental or complicated, there is a sense of restlessness or mental effort in the contemplation of the work. Where the ratios are simple and easy to grasp, not only is a harmonious impression produced, but the mind of the beholder can relax its strain, and fall into a mood of passive receptivity in which the beauty of form has its full effect. To many the monotony of Polyclitus may seem at first uninteresting; his work, so far as we can judge it from extant copies, has neither the ennobling ideals or ethical conception of Polygnotus and Phidias, nor the subtle characterisation and psychological interest of the masters of the fourth century. But no one who will resign himself for a time to the contemplation of a Polyclitan statue can fail to find in it that restful harmony and self-contained perfection that are, perhaps, the most characteristic qualities of Greek sculpture.

If the monotony of Polyclitus is to some extent borne out by our evidence as to the *Doryphorus*, a great surprise awaits us when we come to consider his other famous athletic statue, the *Diadumenus*; for the extant copies of this work vary among themselves in a remarkable way, and it is by no means easy to decide

PLATE XXXV

DIADUMENUS, AFTER POLYCLITUS, FROM DELOS

*To face p.* 124

PLATE XXXVI

To face p. 125

HEAD OF DIADUMENUS, IN DRESDEN

which of them is most faithful to their common
original. The statue represents a youth somewhat
younger than the *Doryphorus*. His position is similar
in the slow advance indicated by the position of the
legs; but it is less appropriate here; for the athlete
has both arms raised in the act of binding around
his head the flat fillet over which the victor's wreath
is to be placed. This motive gives an admirable
opportunity for a display of the beautiful proportions
of the upper part of the torso. If we had no other
copy of this statue besides that from Vaison in the
British Museum, it would be classified without hesitation as similar in type and style to the *Doryphorus*;
it shows the same heavy forms, the same clearly defined
muscles and even the face and hair are not dissimilar,
allowing for the effect of the fillet. But other copies
of the statue vary very greatly from this. Notably
two heads at Cassel and Dresden (the latter here reproduced)—to take the most extreme examples first—
show great softness of marble technique in the treatment of the face, and freedom in the hair, which
stands out from the head and wells out strongly
from beneath the fillet; indeed, this Dresden head
was actually quoted by Conze, in contrast to the
Bologna head of the *Lemnia*, as an example of Attic
as opposed to Argive technique. This comparison of

Conze's is instructive, not because he or any one else
would now maintain it, but because it records an observation quite sound in itself, the Argive quality to be
seen in the *Lemnia*, and the Attic character to be
recognised in the Dresden *Diadumenus*. Nevertheless
the Dresden head is evidently not an independent
work, but a mere variation upon a Polyclitan type;
it has many of the characteristics, as to proportions
and structure, which we see in the *Doryphorus*; its
difference is mainly in texture and treatment of surface. There are two possible explanations of this fact.
The one is that Polyclitus himself changed his style
in his later years, under direct or indirect Attic
influence, and that the *Diadumenus* is an example of
this later style; the other, that the original of the
*Diadumenus* was not dissimilar in style to the *Doryphorus*, but that various copyists, especially in trans-
lating it into marble, have softened its character under
Attic influence. In order to decide between these two
alternatives, it is necessary to consider the evidence of
other copies. One of these, found in Delos, is most
instructive. It is, in the first place, of Hellenistic date,
not Roman, like most of the other copies; and it is
evidently a much freer copy than some of them. In the
body as well as in the head, we find here a substitution
of far slighter proportions and softer modelling for those

PLATE XXXVII

HEAD OF DIADUMENUS, IN BRITISH MUSEUM

*To face p.* 127

we have learnt to associate with Polyclitus; and the substitution is doubtless made in accordance with the taste of the period. Yet another variation is to be seen in a head found in Greece and acquired by the British Museum (*see* Pl. XXXVII). Here the imitation of bronze technique is visible in the clear-cut outlines of brow and eyelids, and in the minute wiry lines of the hair. The expression and character of the head also are nearer to those of the *Doryphorus* than is the case with the Dresden head. But the hair, though not treated in the marble style of that head, resembles it in the vigorous way in which it stands out from under the fillet, in contrast to the hair of the *Doryphorus*, which projects very little at any point. On all this evidence it is difficult to resist the conclusion that the *Diadumenus* of Polyclitus did show a distinct advance upon the *Doryphorus*, especially in the greater freedom of its treatment of the hair, and the somewhat slighter proportions, and the British Museum head would seem to be the most faithful copy of the original. At the same time we must admit that later copyists sometimes carried this Atticising influence much further than Polyclitus himself had done; while others, such as the author of the Vaison statue, seem to have imported into the *Diadumenus* something of that heaviness which was regarded, mainly because of the *Doryphorus*, as charac-

teristic of Polyclitus. In any case, the variation
between the copies is a warning against any too confident inferences as to an original, where less evidence
exists for its reconstruction.

Two more examples of the *Diadumenus* type may also
be mentioned here. One is a terra-cotta, published in
the " Journal of Hellenic Studies," Plate LXI. (vol. vi.).
This is clearly derived from the work of Polyclitus, but
closely assimilated in modelling to the *Hermes* of
Praxiteles—so closely indeed, that its genuineness has
been suspected. Whether an ancient or a modern copy,
it shows us how a type created by one artist can be
modified to conform to the style of a later master.
Another, known as the *Diadumenus Farnese*, is in the
British Museum ; this is not derived from the work of
Polyclitus ; its position, style, and proportions are all
of them Attic, and it has by some been identified as a
copy of a *Boy Binding on a Fillet*, made by Phidias.
The subject is a common one at all periods of Greek
sculpture ; and the *Farnese* statue is mentioned here,
not because it has any relation to Polyclitus, but
because some confusion exists upon the matter.

We have a record of several portraits of victorious
athletes by Polyclitus, including the early works which,
as we have seen, date the beginning of his artistic career
well before the middle of the fifth century. The bases

PLATE XXXVIII

"WESTMACOTT ATHLETE," IN BRITISH
MUSEUM

*To face p.* 129

of several of these have been found at Olympia and the
marks for fixing the feet of the statue show that in
them also, as in the *Doryphorus* and *Diadumenus*,
Polyclitus adopted the position with one foot advanced
and planted firmly on the ground, the other merely
touching it with the toes. Some have gone further,
and noting that the left foot was advanced in the
*Cyniscus*, propose to identify copies of that statue in
a figure of a *Boy crowning himself*, that has survived
in several examples, notably in the Westmacott *Athlete*
of the British Museum. That this statue is of Polyclitan
character is obvious; the close clinging hair in small
wavy locks also resembles that of the *Doryphorus*.
But the slender forms, the exaggeration of the attitude,
especially in the droop of the head and the sinking of
the right hip, do not seem probable in a work by the
master himself, much less in the earliest of his recorded
works. It seems more probable that we see here a
work of one of his scholars or successors, imitating very
closely his earlier style. There is a whole series of such
later Polyclitan works, mostly more slender in form
and more sentimental in character, of which a well-
known example is the *Idolino* at Florence. There
are also several heads of athletes in our museums
which were evidently made under the influence of
Polyclitus, but show too strong an individuality to be

attributed to him.  One of the finest of these is a
marble head recently in the possession of Dr. Philip
Nelson, and now in America.  This shows all the indications of derivation from a bronze original, especially
in the clear outline of lips and brow, and the indication
of the inset border of the eyelids.  The hair is, however, treated with much more freedom than in the
*Doryphorus ;* and there is an amount of expression in
the face far beyond what we see in Polyclitan heads,
even, perhaps, a tendency to sentiment.  There is a
remarkable similarity between this head and that of
one of the *Wounded Amazons,* which we must consider
soon.  Furtwängler would attribute both to Cresilas,
known to us as the author of the portrait of Pericles ;
possibly both may be the work of a sculptor more
directly dependent on Polyclitus than seems probable
in the case of Cresilas, though Furtwängler infers that
Cresilas worked with Polyclitus at Argos in his later
years.  All this is problematical.  But the fact is clear
that we have in this head the work of a sculptor of
strong originality, carrying on the traditions established
by Polyclitus.  Another head, in the Louvre, found at
Beneventum, has the great advantage of being itself a
bronze and not a translation into marble.  In it we see
the Polyclitan tradition softened and modified ; the
proportions are slighter, especially in the lower part of

PLATE XXXIX

HEAD OF ATHLETE ("NELSON HEAD")

*To face p.* 130

PLATE XL

BRONZE HEAD FROM BENEVENTUM, IN THE LOUVRE

*Between pp.* 130 *and* 131

PLATE XLI

AMAZON, AFTER POLYCLITUS, IN LANSDOWNE
HOUSE          *To face p. 131*

the face, and the hair much more varied. But the beauty
of the work is much greater than in later and more
mechanical copies ; and it gives one, in many ways, a
more satisfactory notion of the attainments of the
Argive school of bronze-workers in the age of Polyclitus
or his immediate successors.

Another series of extant statues that can be associated
with Polyclitus are connected with the following tale
told by Pliny. "The most famous artists, though born
in different ages, entered into contest with one another
in making *Amazons*. When these were dedicated in
the temple of Artemis at Ephesus, it was decided to
choose out the most admirable by the verdict of the
artists themselves who were present ; and this proved to
be the one each had put second to his own, namely, that
of Polyclitus ; the next was that of Phidias, the third
of Cresilas the Cydonian, the fourth of Phradmon." [1]
The story is of little historical value, and is not even
consistent with itself; but the *Amazons* at Ephesus
attributed to these masters certainly existed, for some of
them are elsewhere referred to, notably that of Phidias,
selected by Lucian for the " setting of the mouth and
the neck," and that of Cresilas, described as " wounded."
There are many statues of *Amazons* preserved in our
museums, and some of these have nothing to do with the

[1] The obvious mistake in Pliny is here corrected.

Ephesian series.   But there are two types in particular,
both representing wounded Amazons, which evidently
have a close relation to each other ; and one of these is
so evidently Polyclitan in character that there has been
no hesitation among archæologists as to its identification.   A beautiful copy of this Polyclitan *Amazon*
exists in Lansdowne House and is here reproduced,
both the whole figure and the head on a larger scale.
Here we see the characteristic Polyclitan attitude in the
walking position, with the right foot advanced and
firmly planted on the ground, the left raised.   But a
new motive is introduced in the pillar on which the left
arm rests, though this rest hardly seems to affect the
general pose, and is even, perhaps, inconsistent with it.
The right arm is raised and the hand touches the head,
thus offering variety of composition and an excellent
opportunity, as in the *Diadumenus*, for displaying the
modelling of the chest.   The head, like that of the
*Doryphorus*, is turned towards the advanced right leg ;
it is more bent than in the *Doryphorus*, thus resembling
the Westmacott *Athlete;* but here the motive is
evidently to be found in the physical exhaustion or
depression also indicated by the motive of leaning
upon a support.   It is not until we examine the statue
more closely that we notice a deep incised wound beside
the right breast.   The Amazon is indeed standing

PLATE XLII

HEAD OF AMAZON, IN LANSDOWNE HOUSE

*To face p.* 132

in such a position as would strain the muscles around the wound and so increase its pain; and it has even been suggested for this reason that the wound cannot have existed in the original, but was introduced into extant copies in imitation of another statue which did represent a wounded Amazon. This suggestion can hardly be maintained, in view of the agreement of all extant copies; but it would seem that Polyclitus, in his desire to choose a beautiful and effective pose, has ignored the physical effect of the wound he has represented. Thus his work is in direct contrast with that of Cresilas, who was famous for his representation of a man fainting from his wounds—not to speak of his *Wounded Amazon*, to which we must return directly—and even of Pythagoras, whose vivid rendering of the *Wounded Philoctetes* made those who saw it feel his pain. The contrast is probably characteristic both of the master and of the Argive school to which he belongs. His object is not to represent the psychological or even the physical interest of a wounded figure, but rather to produce a perfect type of Amazon, just as his *Doryphorus* and *Diadumenus* offered perfect types of athletes; and the wound is a mere incident. As such a typical figure, the *Amazon* is admirable, and one easily understands the verdict on the Ephesian statues. For beauty of pose and of proportions it

cannot be surpassed.   The drapery of the short chiton,
secured only on one shoulder and round the waist, shows
the same predilection for breaking up the whole into
clear and distinct masses that we see in the Polyclitan
treatment of the muscular structure of an athlete; and
here the effect, in the simple disposition of the central
part drawn up through the girdle, and subordinate
pieces with folds curving up to it on each side, is most
effective.   The head, especially in the Lansdowne copy,
is also very beautiful in proportions.    The hair is
simply treated in wavy masses, and it projects enough
to shadow the forehead and cheeks; eyes and mouth
alike are given a slight droop which suggests, delicately,
something of pain and weariness, without any pathetic
exaggeration.   In all alike we see the Polyclitan characteristics of harmony and restraint, which make his work
not, indeed, imposing at first sight, but satisfying to
those who will attune themselves to his mode, and give
themselves time to appreciate the artistic character
of his work.

The other *Wounded Amazon* [1] known to us by copies
need only be quoted here to emphasise by its contrast
the qualities we have noticed in the Polyclitan statues.
In this other *Amazon* the wound (or rather wounds, for

[1] *See* my " Handbook of Greek Sculpture," Fig. 77, and the head
of Fig. 78.

there are two), far from being incidental, is made
the chief motive of the whole composition. She has
loosened her chiton from her right shoulder, and holds
it with her hand away from the wound, towards which
she is looking down with an expression of pathos,
admirably rendered, but in contrast to the restraint of
the Polyclitan head. The drapery is much less simple
than in the Polyclitan figure, and less clearly arranged;
the hair also is a little more elaborately treated, though
similar in character. The whole effect is softer and
more feminine, as if the artist had tried to excite the
pity of the spectator by not dwelling too much on the
virile qualities of these Amazonian warriors. The
position of the legs is practically that of the Polyclitan
*Amazon* reversed; but the head being still inclined
towards her right, the effect of the position is very
different. It is impossible to regard this statue as an
independent variation on the same motive; it is evidently derived from the work of Polyclitus with intentional modifications. It is hardly too much to say, as
some archæologists have done, that it is almost a
conscious protest against Polyclitus' treatment of the
theme, especially as regards his ignoring of the wound.
The statue must then be attributed to an artist of
originality, working under the influence of the Argive
master. This is not the place to discuss who that

artist was. Furtwängler, emphasising the description
of Cresilas' *Amazon* as wounded, thinks the statue is
his, and infers from this and other evidence that
Cresilas migrated to Argos and fell under the influence
of Polyclitus in his later years. The *Amazon* and the
*Head of an Athlete* discussed above (Pl. XXXIX.) are
so much alike that they must almost certainly be attributed to the same sculptor, whether that sculptor be
Cresilas or another. Perhaps, in view of his obvious
dependence upon Polyclitus, it is more probable that
both should be attributed to a sculptor who, like the
Argive Phradmon, finds his natural place among the
scholars of Polyclitus. They show a modification of
the severe Polyclitan forms not only to slighter proportions and softer modelling, but also towards a
pathos of expression which another great follower of
the Argive tradition, Scopas, was to carry much further
in a later generation.

So far our estimate of the artistic attainments of
Polyclitus has been based mainly upon extant statues
which may be derived from his work. But we must
not forget that his athletic statues only showed one
side, though perhaps the most characteristic side, of his
activity. He also made statues of gods and heroes—
notably a *Heracles*, whose head is probably preserved
for us in more than one copy. But the most famous of

all his works, the one that came into the mind of any
Greek when the name of Polyclitus was mentioned, was
the colossal *Hera* at Argos, made of gold and ivory.
This statue, as has already been stated, belongs to the
later years of his career, for the temple in which it was
placed was built to replace the one burnt in 424 B.C.
It represented the goddess seated upon a throne, with a
high crown upon her head wrought with figures of the
Graces and the Hours; in one hand she held a pome-
granate, in the other a sceptre surmounted by a cuckoo.
From what we know of the Argive ritual of the goddess,
we learn that she was especially worshipped as the bride
whose marriage with Zeus was annually celebrated at
her great festival, and who annually renewed her vir-
ginity by bathing in a sacred spring. It was probably
as the maiden bride that Polyclitus portrayed her, and
such a subject would suit well his preference for youthful
forms and physical beauty. Of the statue itself we
have no extant copies; Roman coins upon which it is
represented show us little that we could not gather
from the description of Pausanias; and although the
head of the goddess appears upon contemporary coins
of Argos, these merely give us the type under which the
goddess of the city was worshipped, and cannot be
regarded as direct copies of the statue. There is,
indeed, good reason for believing that Polyclitus fixed

the type of *Hera* for all later art very much as Phidias
fixed that of *Zeus;* and there are some extant heads of
*Hera* which closely resemble what we can recognise as
his work in other cases.   Chief among these is the
Farnese *Hera*, a very beautiful and queenly, yet youthful face; the shape and build of the head are like those
of Polyclitan statues, and the severe dignity and simplicity of modelling also recalls his style.   The head is
the subject of an interesting study by Brunn, in which
he points out how the square and broad forehead adds
to the majesty of the head, and how it shows a passive
and receptive nature rather than the actively intellectual
type that characterises *Apollo* or *Athena.*   Another
head, which has been generally recognised as Polyclitan,
though it was thought to be male, is in the British
Museum.   It is published by Professor Waldstein in
the "Journal of Hellenic Studies" (xxi., Plate III.), as
a copy of the Argive *Hera.*   But in the absence of the
high crown it is difficult to prove any so direct relation,
though as a Polyclitan female head it may help us,
with the *Amazon* and the Farnese *Hera,* to realise what
the Argive statue by Polyclitus may have been.   The
American excavations at the Heraeum have also brought
to light some architectural and other sculptures that
must date from the time when Polyclitus was making
the great statue.   They show in many ways Polyclitan

characteristics, but combine them with other qualities, especially in the treatment of drapery, which show that the influence of the Attic artists employed under Pericles had spread even to Argos. This need not surprise us, if we admit that Polyclitus himself fell under the same influence in his later years.

It is, however, fortunate that our evidence as to the work of Polyclitus is fullest in the case of those athletic statues which were the most distinctive products of his art, and which exercised the greatest influence on his successors.

# CHAPTER VI

## PRAXITELES

In Phidias we have seen the master whose work has won for Greek sculpture the most enthusiastic admiration among modern artists and critics; in Polyclitus, the sculptor whose formal perfection and technical skill were chosen by at least one school of ancient critics as the highest attainments of Greek art. Praxiteles, on the other hand, was probably, in popular estimation of his own and later times, the most famous of all Greek sculptors. The tales about his *Aphrodite* of Cnidus and his *Eros* of Parium or of Thespiæ attest a general appreciation and even a sentimental devotion such as was hardly accorded to the works of any other ancient sculptor. The sensuous beauty of form, the facile and sweeping lines of his composition, the personal and individual charm of his statues all combined to make his works the most highly prized in the Græco-Roman age. Horace's prescription for literary work applied then to art also—

*Non satis est pulchra esse poemata ; dulcia sunto*
*Et quocunque volent animum auditoris agunto.*

Praxiteles is described as the man who " in the highest
degree infused into marble the emotions of the soul "—
not, indeed, the passion and intensity which we see in
the work of Scopas, but the softer moods more pleasing
to the taste of the cultured amateur. For this reason
the adjective Praxitelean has almost become a commonplace, a synonym for easy and graceful beauty of form.
In modern days a kind of reaction has set in against this
high estimate of Praxiteles. The critic of to-day finds
it easy enough to admire the strenuous accuracy of
archaic or transitional art, even if it produce a harsh
or uncouth result; he can also appreciate the
dramatic vigour and intensity of expression which the
Pergamenes learnt from Scopas. But the beauty and
moderation of Praxiteles, more truly Hellenic in character than either, often does not appeal so much to
the modern imagination, just as, in literature, the
somewhat similar qualities shown by the art of Sophocles not infrequently fail to move modern readers,
who are ready enough to recognise the grandeur of
Æschylus or the subtlety and pathos of Euripides.
It may be contended that this very fact shows that the
artist or poet in question was rather for an age than for
all time, since his work, to be fully appreciated, requires

some historical imagination, and some familiarity with
the spirit and conditions of the period.   For this very
reason, however, the study of his works is most instructive, and helps us to understand the thought and history
of his day.   It is not, however, this difficulty of appreciation of the original work of the master himself that
is mainly responsible for the current view of Praxiteles.
Since he was the most popular of all Greek sculptors,
his work naturally came to be most frequently imitated,
and the imitators, consulting their own taste and that
of their patrons, often reproduced and exaggerated the
less admirable qualities of the originals, the grace and
ease of pose and composition, the softness of flesh, the
sentimentality of expression, and failed to realise or to
reproduce the breadth and nobility of type and conception which were probably to be seen in most of the
master's own works.   It is here that the discovery of
an undoubted original from his hand, even if it be only
one of his minor works, has proved invaluable to us.
In future all study of the works of Praxiteles must
begin with the *Hermes* at Olympia.

What we know of Praxiteles from external sources is
but little.   None of his works can be exactly dated,
but they all fit in with most probability to the time
immediately before the middle of the fourth century;
thus he was approximately a contemporary of Scopas.

PLATE XLIII

HERMES, BY PRAXITELES, AT OLYMPIA

*To face p.* 143

There is, indeed, no chronological evidence to place the one master before the other. But Praxiteles seems to come earlier in the development of sculpture, and his work was rather the perfection of what preceded than the origin of what was to follow. He was an Athenian, and he followed throughout the traditions of the Attic school, which often claimed him as its greatest and most representative master. He is said to have been the pupil of Cephisodotus, who was probably either his father or his elder brother. The most interesting stories about him refer to his relations with the famous Phryne, the most beautiful among women. He gave her what he himself esteemed the best of his works, the *Eros* which she dedicated at Thespiæ. He also made a statue of her, which was set up at the same place, and another for Delphi, and she is said to have served as the model for the most famous of his statues, the *Aphrodite* of Cnidus. His favourite material was marble, both that of Paros, of which the Olympian *Hermes* is made, and the no less beautiful marble of Pentelicus, which is said to have been used for the Cnidian goddess. The material was best suited for the exquisite modulation of surface and delicate play of light and shade which we find in his work.

The statue of *Hermes* carrying the infant Dionysus was found by the German excavators in the Heræum

at Olympia, just below the spot where Pausanias had
seen it more than seventeen centuries before.  He
describes it as an original by Praxiteles, and there is no
reason for doubting the correctness of the attribution.
This is the only example in which we actually possess a
statue which is attested by direct evidence to be an
original by one of the great sculptors of Greece.  We
have, of course, numerous architectural sculptures, such
as those of the Parthenon or the heads from the temple
of Athena Alea at Tegea, which were seen by Pausanias where they were subsequently discovered, and
which may be assigned with some confidence to the
influence, if not to the hand, of the sculptors employed
on the temple ; and we have several statues in museums
or private collections which have been claimed, on
internal evidence, as originals by Greek masters.  But
in these cases there is often room for difference of
opinion ; and an example like the *Hermes*, to which we
can refer such doubtful cases for comparison, is of
incalculable service to the historical study of art as
well as to its appreciation.

Hermes is represented by the sculptor as standing
with the child Dionysus supported on his left arm.
This left arm rests upon a tree trunk, partly enveloped
by the chlamys of the god, which has fallen over it.
Thus an extra support is provided, which enables the

figure, whose weight is mostly carried by the right leg, to assume the graceful and easy curve characteristic of Praxiteles and of his successors. His head is slightly turned towards the child, but not so as to look straight at it; his right hand is raised, and is usually restored, in accordance with later representations that are clearly reminiscent of this statue, as holding up a bunch of grapes, towards which the child is reaching out its hand. An alternative suggestion, supported also by some later variations, is that the right arm of Hermes was resting on a sceptre or a long caduceus. Whichever solution we may accept, it is evident from the position and the expression of the god that the subject is not treated after the manner of what may be called mythological genre, a manner exemplified by a later group, made under Praxitelean influence, of a bearded satyr or silenus dangling a bunch of grapes to amuse the infant Bacchus. Here the interest lies in the action and in its treatment. In the *Hermes*, on the other hand, the action is subordinated, and both child and plaything, if such existed, are to be regarded merely as attributes, the interest being centred in the personality and mood of the god. This does not mean that Hermes is a mere abstraction, a representation of the idea of the protector and nurturer of youth (κουροτρόφος). Such a description might suit, perhaps, the *Eirene* or

K

Cephisodotus, a work of fifth-century character.   What
Praxiteles has done—and it is characteristic of his
art—is to take this mythological conception and to
embody it in a clearly expressed and individual personality.   Such is the sympathetic power of the artist
that it is impossible, when we look at his *Hermes*, not
to realise the genial and human character with which
he has endowed the god.   If Phidias " added something
to the accepted religion " by ennobling the current
conception of the gods, and by raising those who saw
his statues into a diviner atmosphere, Praxiteles also
brought the gods nearer to men by making them more
human.   We feel this above all in the *Hermes*.   He is
not looking straight at the child, but away past him ;
his eyes are not wide open, but as if resting, without
concentration, upon some object not far away.   The
whole expression is one of rest and reverie, rather than
of any definite activity either physical or intellectual.
Body and face alike are those of a young man of perfect physical and mental development, but not unduly
trained or specialised ; the forms throughout are far
removed from the over-soft, almost effeminate modelling
that we find in many imitations or copies of the work
of Praxiteles.   The position of the figure also, though
the extra support under the left elbow gives it an ease
and grace beyond what we find in fifth-century sculp-

PLATE XLIV

HEAD OF HERMES, BY PRAXITELES

*To face p.* 146

ture, which only gives variety by the varying amount
of weight thrown on the two legs, has nothing of the
affectation of a somewhat similar pose in later art. We
see a healthy and vigorous nature in a moment of
relaxation, not a morbid or indolent one in its habitual
attitude; Hermes rests, but he does not loll. What
is, however, more characteristic of the work of Praxiteles as we see it in the *Hermes* is the wonderful facility
and truth of the modelling, the distinction of the
features, the easy sweep of all the lines and surfaces of
face and figure, and, combined with these, a treatment of the surface which gives to it the apparent
warmth and elasticity of flesh. There are only very
few pieces of sculpture surviving from Greek times
which have this last quality in a degree approaching
that in which it may be seen in the *Hermes*, and these
have almost all been claimed by one authority or
another as originals from the hand of Praxiteles;
among them are the Petworth *Aphrodite*, the Aberdeen *Head* in the British Museum, and the *Eubuleus*
from Eleusis. The similarity of the impression produced by all these is partly due to the good preservation
of the original surface; but that surface certainly shows
the careful and beautiful treatment of marble that is
peculiarly characteristic of Praxiteles and his school.
The treatment of the surface is, however, to be dis-

tinguished from the style of the modelling, which is
by no means identical in all the works just mentioned.
Even those who attribute them all to Praxiteles assert
that they show the variety of the master's attainments—
a somewhat precarious argument when their attribution
to him is mainly dependent upon internal evidence from
their style.

This, however, is a matter to which we must return
later.  In the *Hermes* the nude parts are treated with
simplicity and directness, but with wonderful subtlety
and delicacy in the transitions, and a play of light and
shade on the polished and transparent surface such as
is almost entirely lost in a cast, though it may be
appreciated to some extent in a good photograph.
The hair is apparently only roughly blocked out, when
one examines it in detail; but the general effect, when
seen from a short distance, gives the most admirable
impression of texture; this is due partly to the roughness of the surface, as contrasted with the smoothness
of the skin, but more still to the masterly manner in
which the separate masses are designed and struck out;
we have here no attempt, as in fifth-century art, to
imitate the actual form of hair, but a frankly impressionist treatment.  The drapery, again, in its marvellously skilful rendering of folds and texture, is such
as almost to deceive the eye; it is difficult to believe

that we have merely a piece of marble before us. There
is not so clear a system of folds as in the sculptures of
the Parthenon ; but while their arrangement looks at
first sight more spontaneous and accidental, the careful
avoidance of anything exaggerated or awkward, such as
we usually find in earlier or later attempts at realism,
shows again the subtle discrimination and inimitable
technical skill of Praxiteles. Perhaps the sense of texture is nowhere seen so clearly as in the right foot and
sandal, only to be appreciated properly in the presence
of the original itself—the contrast between the leather
straps and the live skin beneath them. But all these
things, though each contributes its part to the general
effect, are but details. What one feels as one looks at the
*Hermes* is the wonderful combination of strength and
grace in the figure, the fulness of life that animates it,
the intellectual quality of the face, the clearly realised
personality of the god, as expressed in his mood
of reverie; and if, in copies of other works by
Praxiteles, one cannot recognise these qualities, or can
only see a faint reflection of them, this *Hermes* helps
us to appreciate how much the copyist has lost of the
spiritual and intellectual character of the original, as
well as of its technical skill in execution.

So far we have been considering the *Hermes* by
itself, as a characteristic conception of Greek art in the

fourth century, and as a trustworthy example of the style of Praxiteles. But it also takes its place in several series of sculptures that reach both backwards and forwards far beyond his period. As regards subject, we have already noticed, for the sake of contrast, the later groups of *Silenus and the Infant Bacchus*, in which the treatment is more or less dramatic, and the interest lies in the action of the two figures. There are also earlier examples of a figure of a god or goddess carrying a child ; and among these one naturally selects for comparison with the *Hermes* the *Eirene and Plutus*, *Peace carrying the Child Wealth*, which was made by Cephisodotus, either the father or the elder brother of Praxiteles. A copy of this work exists at Munich, and shows the severe and dignified traditions of the fifth century ; it was in bronze, and of course the copy may have lost some of the qualities of the original; but it foreshadows but little the life and warmth that Praxiteles has put into his work ; it is, in fact, an uninspired allegory, though the tradition of the great age gives it a beauty and dignity of form that is rarely missing in works made under the Phidian influence. It is true that this *Eirene* of Cephisodotus probably belongs in date to the fourth century ; but it was before that century had developed its characteristic tendencies. The group, however, if group it may be called, may have suggested

to Praxiteles the composition of his *Hermes;* we have,
indeed, a more direct anticipation in a *Hermes nursing
the Infant Dionysus*, which Pliny attributes to Cephisodotus, if we are to trust Pliny's statement; but it is
possible the compiler may have confused some reference
to the two works.  In any case, Praxiteles has made the
subject his own by the freshness and originality of his
treatment.  And what is true of the composition and
subject is true also of the proportions of the body and
the character of the head.  In both alike we may recognise the Attic tradition which may be traced back to
Alcamenes and Myron ; yet this fact merely emphasises
the regular and organic development of Greek sculpture,
and in no way detracts from the originality and
individuality of Praxiteles.

The *Hermes,* though recorded by Pausanias and
invaluable to us as an identified statue, was by no means
among the best-known works of Praxiteles.  These seem
to have been sought rather amid the cycle of Aphrodite
and Dionysus, deities more identified with human
passions and delights.  There was more scope here for
that "infusion of the passions of the soul into marble"
which Diodorus attributes to Praxiteles.  This does not
mean that Praxiteles, like his great contemporary Scopas
preferred to represent figures in violent or passionate
action or emotion ; his gods and goddesses mostly repre-

sent the passive and receptive nature rather than the active or passionate ; his methods are more subtle and less forcible.   The most famous of the works of Praxiteles—perhaps the most famous statue of the ancient world—was the *Aphrodite* which he made for the Cnidians, and which was set up in her temple close to the two harbours of Cnidus.   This statue is reproduced on the coins of the city, and by their help it has been possible to recognise extant copies of it, one in the Vatican and one in Munich.   The photograph of the Vatican copy here reproduced is taken from a cast ; those familiar with the original in the Vatican may be confused by the tin drapery placed around its legs. There are also several other copies or variants of the head alone, some superior in workmanship to either of the complete statues.   It is somewhat difficult to determine whether all or any of these are to be regarded as copies of the Cnidian statue.   Praxiteles had many pupils and imitators whose work came very near to his own in character, though they probably missed his inimitable finish and distinction ; and it is probable that some of these heads, especially those of Greek period, are to be regarded rather as variations upon the type which Praxiteles had established, while one of them, the Petworth head, is regarded by Furtwängler as an original by Praxiteles himself.   We may make use of

PLATE XLV

APHRODITE OF CNIDUS, AFTER PRAXITELES, IN VATICAN
(FROM A CAST)

To face p. 152

all this evidence, with due reserve, as giving us a general notion of the *Aphrodite* of Praxiteles, though we cannot be sure what details are derived from the Cnidian statue; and we must also remember that several other statues of the goddess by Praxiteles are recorded, although none of them approached the Cnidian in fame. As to the pose and motive of the statue the extant copies give us sufficient evidence. The goddess was represented as nude; and an explanation of her nudity was supplied by the indications that she is preparing for the bath; her garment is just slipping down from her left hand on to a vase that stands beside her. She holds her right hand in front of her body, as if half consciously shrinking from the complete unveiling of her beauty. The motive is in all probability a new one, and is certainly characteristic. The representation of a goddess entirely undraped was probably in itself a new departure. It is true that figures of nude goddesses, possibly of Oriental origin, are found in the earliest time of Greek art; but these were of symbolic character, and show no attempt to realise the divinity of their subject. In the fifth century, so far as we know, no statue of a nude goddess was made; but, if it had been, we may be sure that she would have been represented as "naked and unashamed." The feeling of Greeks of the fourth century about the matter is illustrated by the tale—

whether true or invented does not matter — that
Praxiteles made two statues of *Aphrodite*, one draped
and one nude; and the people of Cos, who were given
the choice, preferred the draped statue for its dignity
and modesty; the nude one, which became immensely
more famous, was acquired by the Cnidians.  Modesty
is essentially a human rather than a divine virtue.  But
the Cnidian *Aphrodite* certainly does not transcend it by
her divinity.  In her the humanity of the Praxitelean
conception of the gods is emphasised.  The gods are
constantly represented nude in the fourth-century art
because the practice of athletic exercises had accustomed
the Greeks to see men and boys constantly without any
clothes on; the more august and dignified conceptions
of the fifth century were more often embodied in fully
draped figures.  This absence of drapery in fourth-
century representations of the gods is, therefore, an
example of the tendency which we notice on every side
towards bringing the gods nearer to the feelings and
habits of our common humanity.  With this statue of
a goddess it is otherwise.  Whatever be the tales about
Phryne, how she put off all her clothes and loosed
her hair and bathed before the whole assembly at a
festival, a nude female figure, whether woman or goddess,
was evidently regarded as requiring some explanation or
special motive, not as a common type of everyday life.

It is said that the unconventional act of Phryne suggested to Praxiteles his Cnidian goddess, and to Apelles his no less famous picture of Aphrodite arising from the sea. Considering that Greek sculptors appear not to have been in the habit of posing models, the story is perhaps probable, though Praxiteles, who was a favoured lover of Phryne and also made a portrait statue of her, doubtless had other opportunities for observing her beauty. All this emphasises the individuality and clearly realised personality of the goddess, her human moods and consciousness. But the restraint and good feeling of the fourth century prevented any such obvious coquetry as we see in later imitations of the Praxitelean statue such as the *Venus de' Medici*, whose gesture seems to imply a consciousness of observation, and to emphasise the nudity it seems to hide, almost as in primitive Græco-Oriental images the same gesture is used as a symbolic accentuation of sex. There is nothing of this in the Cnidian figure; her expression and gesture alike suggest the absence rather than the presence of any observer; she shrinks not from human eyes, but, as one used to the decent veil of drapery, from exposing her body even to the breezes and to the sunlight. This, it may be said, is not a divine conception, nor even a noble conception of womanhood. But, such as it is, it is treated with delicacy as well as consummate skill.

The position and the modelling of the figure are distinguished by the same qualities which we noticed in the *Hermes*, though here we have only copies to deal with, and therefore cannot expect to find the same matchless subtlety in the treatment of the marble. But even in these copies we can see something of the same ease and flow of line, which justifies and illustrates Lucian's enthusiastic description of the exquisite curves and outlines of body and limbs. The figure is not, as in so many Praxitelean statues, represented as supported partly on one elbow, though something of the same effect is given by the drapery that falls from the hand on to the vase; but the delicate poise of the figure and the strong curve of the median line are as characteristic. The form of the body, as Lucian says, hits the happy mean between too slight or too soft and heavy proportions; but they have a breadth, simplicity and dignity of type, especially in the modelling of the chest, which contrasts strongly with the too rounded and narrow forms of later *Aphrodites*. The head, of which we have more and better copies, shows the delicate oval characteristic of Attic art. The hair, which frames the high triangular space of the forehead, has a wavy texture and a roughness of surface which, as in the *Hermes*, suggests rather than reproduces the texture of the material, and is contrasted with the

PLATE XLVI

HEAD OF APHRODITE. "KAUFMANN HEAD." AFTER *ANTIKE DENKMAELER*, I., XLI

*To face p.* 157

smooth and elastic skin of the face; it is this latter
above all that in the Petworth head shows the same
warmth and life that we noticed in the *Hermes*, and
that has led to its being claimed as an original work of
Praxiteles. But the life is above all in the expression.
This may be appreciated partly from the head of the
Vatican statue, partly from the Kaufmann head in
Berlin, which appears to be a good copy of the original.
The treatment of the eyes, on which the expression to
a great extent depends, has lost much of its delicacy,
as was to be expected; but we can judge of it from
the *Hermes* and from the Petworth head. They were
long and not widely open, the lower lid, especially at
the outside, almost fading into invisibility; and the
resultant vagueness of outline contributes to the soft
dreamy expression, as of Lely's "sleepy eye that
speaks the melting soul." Yet there is nothing here of
languor or voluptuousness; the expression is rather of
innocence and simplicity that accords with the youthful
and rounded contour of the face, and that contrasts
with the Petworth head, which seems to be of maturer
age. The half-open lips add to the effect, which gives
the impression of a sensitive and receptive nature rather
than of any strong emotion. Above all, there is a grace
and charm about both face and figure which are due in
part to the avoidance of anything extreme or excessive,

as well as to the easy flow of line and to the beauty of the physical type. Praxiteles could make marble live and breathe, but he did not, nor did he attempt to make it pulsate with passion like the works of Scopas.

The Cnidian *Aphrodite* was only one of several representations of the goddess which we know to have been made by Praxiteles ; it is possible that we possess copies of some of these, but there are no criteria for a certain identification. We have already noticed that many heads of *Aphrodite* of Praxitelean type are known. Among these the Petworth head is not to be regarded as a copy from the Cnidian statue, but is distinguished from it by the less rounded form of the face, and greater accentuation of the features, and also by a heavier roll of flesh round the neck—all of them characteristics which seem to be studied from a model of maturer age. If the head is to be attributed to Praxiteles himself, it certainly belongs, like the *Hermes*, to his later years ; and it may even be suggested that, if Phryne served as his model for *Aphrodite*, this Petworth head may represent her later characteristics, as the Cnidian goddess corresponds to the first bloom of her womanhood. Such a suggestion is not to be pressed in the case of any Greek statue. But from the nature of the case it is more likely to be applicable in the case of a female than of a male figure. In this connection it is to be

PLATE XLVII

HEAD OF APHRODITE (OR PHRYNE), "PETWORTH HEAD"

*To face p.* 158

PLATE XLVIII

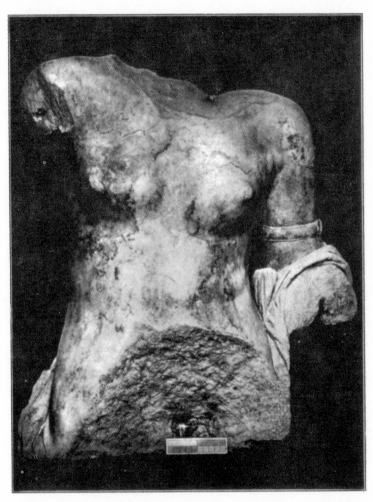

TORSO OF APHRODITE, TYPE OF VENUS OF ARLES, IN ATHENS

*To face p. 159*

remembered that Praxiteles made two portrait statues
of *Phryne* which were set up, one in marble at her native
town of Thespiæ, and the other in gilt bronze at
Delphi. We have no certain criteria by which these
portraits or copies of them may be recognised among
extant statues, and without further information as to
their pose and motive, any such identification can only
be conjectural ; but it has been suggested with some
probability that one of the Praxitelean figures representing a goddess or a woman at her toilet, holding a mirror
in one hand and doing up her hair with the other, may
be derived from the statue of *Phryne*. The type is one
that is familiar with many variations in the sculpture
that owes its inspiration to Praxiteles. The figure is
standing, her drapery fixed in a coil about her waist or
her hips, so as to leave the upper part of her body bare ;
well-known examples are the *Venus* of Arles in the
Louvre and the Townley *Venus* in the British Museum ;
a beautiful example of the torso only is to be seen
in Athens, and is here reproduced. It is broader and
simpler in treatment than the more complete statues,
and the proportions and beauty of form remind us of
the best copies of the Cnidian statue ; indeed, being of
Greek and not Roman workmanship, they may help us
better than those copies to imagine what Praxiteles'
statue may have been. It has been suggested that this

half-draped figure represents an intermediate stage
between the draped goddesses of earlier art and the
completely nude statue of Cnidus; as if Greek sculptors
had hesitated to unveil all the charms of *Aphrodite*,
and had only ventured by slow degrees to remove more
and more of her garments. It may, however, be doubted
whether any such gradual process is either proved or
probable. A figure employed on her toilet, with her
drapery hitched up round her waist, is perhaps less
easy to reconcile with any divine ideal than one with
no clothes at all, and might even be regarded as a
compromise worthy only of the artificial devices of
later Greek art. Without going so far as this, one
may certainly admit that such a figure represents the
goddess under a peculiarly human aspect, and therefore
does not necessarily belong to an earlier type. The per-
sistency with which it is repeated in later art, even in
such variations as the *Aphrodite* of Melos or the *Victory*
of Brescia, shows us its popularity.

The statues of *Eros* made by Praxiteles were hardly
less famous than those of *Aphrodite*. One of these was
set up at Parium, a colony on the sea of Marmora, and
the other at Thespiæ in Bœotia. In both places the
worship of Eros was the chief cult of the town, and
goes back to a very different mythological conception
from that which became current in Greece as the child

and constant companion of Aphrodite. But Praxiteles'
treatment of the subject was calculated to break down
any such distinction. His *Eros* is no august and
mysterious deity; nor is he, on the other hand, the
philosophical impersonation of the force of attraction
in nature dear to mythological theory. He is rather a
beautiful and intensely human personality; the dreamy
youth whose "fancy lightly turns to thoughts of love,"
who shows in his own character the mood of pensive
and vague desire that he inspires in his votaries. Thus
much we may gather from the many copies of a Praxitelean *Eros*, or variations upon it, which we may see in
our museums. The *Eros* of Parium is reproduced on
the coins of the town. The pose of the statue was
similar to that of the *Hermes* and of some other Praxitelean statues that we must notice later on. Eros was
leaning his left elbow on a column, over which his cloak
hung down; the weight of the body was supported on
the right hip, which projected so as to give a strong
curve to the figure; his head was turned to his left,
with a strong upward inclination. As to the Thespian
statue, we have no such certain information. This was
even the more famous of the two. When Praxiteles
had promised to give Phryne the most beautiful of his
works, she made him select it for her himself by means
of a trick, telling him his studio was on fire. He is

L

said to have named as most valuable in his eyes the
*Satyr* and the *Eros;* she chose the *Eros,* and it was
dedicated at Thespiæ, her native town, beside her own
portrait and an *Aphrodite* by Praxiteles.   Many conjectures have been made as to copies of these two
statues among extant works.   It has been suggested,
for example, that the *Eros* of Centocelle, the Genius of
the Vatican, as it is sometimes called, must be a copy
of the Thespian *Eros.*   It is, indeed, the most beautiful
example that we possess of the Praxitelean type, and so
serves better than any other to give us a notion of the
original ; but we have no evidence that in position and
accessories it reproduces the Thespian statue.   In the
fifth century, as we may see on the Parthenon frieze,
Eros was merely a winged boy, without much further
characterisation.   It was Praxiteles who made him the
embodiment of tender sentiment and reverie that is
familiar to us in many variations, and gave him the
soft and delicate forms appropriate to his character,
though not the effeminate type which we find in later
imitations or travesties of Praxitelean art.   Such imitations are as far removed from the Praxitelean *Eros* as are
the similar degradations of the type of the Cnidian
*Aphrodite.*   But he is usually in the fourth century
represented as a youth, almost between boy and man.
The playful baby type that is beloved by Hellenistic

and Renaissance art does not belong to the age of
Praxiteles.

The *Satyr* is coupled with the *Eros* in the story of
Phryne's device. This statue is by general consent
identified with the figure of a satyr preserved to us in
many copies, of which the most familiar is that known
as the Capitoline *Faun*, the best in execution a torso
in the Louvre, which has even been claimed to be the
original. This *Satyr* is in the same position that we
have noticed in the *Hermes* and in the Parian *Eros*,
one elbow being supported on a pillar; but the sides
are in this case inverted, the right elbow giving the
support. The right leg is more bent at the knee, and
the foot is placed just behind the other, so as to make
the pose more of a lounge. This is in accordance with
the character of the half-human, soulless creature that
is here represented with wonderful subtlety and power.
The choice of the subject and its treatment are alike
interesting. The god Dionysus and his rout of dis-
orderly and ecstatic followers, bacchantes and mænads,
satyrs and sileni, had been a theme familiar to Greek
art from the earliest times; but it had been rendered
with a half-comic, half-brutal directness that was in
accordance with the primitive orgies in which these
figures had their origin. In the fifth century there is
more dignity and moderation in such representations;

and the god himself often has a sad or thoughtful
expression, which is probably to be explained with
reference to the deeper meaning of the Bacchic mysteries.    But it was reserved for Praxiteles and Scopas
to find in the attendants of the god a theme of the
highest psychological interest.    We shall see the intensity of orgiastic frenzy in the *Mœnad* of Scopas.
The *Satyr* of Praxiteles, on the other hand, shows the
irresponsible and pleasure-loving nature of the wild
creature of the woods, his indolence and passive enjoy-
ment.    He has been amusing himself with the flute
that he holds in his right hand, and now is content to
be at rest—a charming and graceful figure, free from
all moral or intellectual restraint, a contrast alike to
the sombre and to the enthusiastic sides of the Bacchic
religion.    This is probably the most famous of the
Praxitelean *Satyrs;* but others are recorded and probably preserved in copies.    There was in Athens, in
the same street, a group by Praxiteles of a satyr
pouring a cup of wine for the god ; and this is probably
to be recognised in the graceful figure standing with a
jug in the right hand raised above its head, pouring
wine into a cup held in the left hand.    This satyr
cup-bearer has the Praxitelean qualities of grace in
proportions and flowing modelling; but it resembles
also a well-known athletic figure of the fifth century, of

an athlete anointing himself, standing in much the same position, with his right hand holding the oil-flask above his head. As the *Satyr* is also somewhat simpler and severer in style than other Praxitelean works, it is usually assigned to the earlier years of Praxiteles, while he was still under the influence of his predecessors. Groups of two figures, such as this of Dionysus and the satyr who attends him, became common in later branches of the Praxitelean school. They offer an admirable opportunity for contrast and harmony in the composition and relation of the god and his attendant, as well as for the pleasing variety of their character and mood.

There are none among the gods in whose representation we should expect the art of Praxiteles to find a more congenial task than Apollo and Artemis, and we find accordingly that several statues of these deities are recorded among his works, and that many extant figures of them in our museums are derived more or less directly from him or from his pupils. Of a group of the two with their mother Leto, which he made for Mantinea, only the basis has been found; and to this we must recur later when considering another aspect of his art. Perhaps the best known statue of *Apollo* attributed to him is one of some mythological interest, the *Sauroctonus*, or lizard-slayer. The origin of the type is obscure; but Praxiteles' treatment of it was popular as to be preserved to us in several copies. His *Apollo* is a youthful figure, who leans towards a tree-trunk on which he rests his raised left hand; in his right he holds an arrow as if about to stab at a lizard that runs up the tree. We have, in fact, a serious mythological subject treated as a mere sport or pastime; there is but a slight allusion to the religious type. On the other hand, the artist revels in the grace and beauty of the youthful boyish form, the easy curve of its position and the delicacy of its modelling. It is probable that in the copies of the *Sauroctonus*, as in other figures of *Apollo*, evidently derived from a Praxitelean original, the copyist has exaggerated the softness of the figure almost to effeminacy; but the general character of the statue can hardly be mis-represented.

The statue of *Artemis Brauronia* on the Acropolis at Athens is also recorded among the works of Praxi-teles. If we accept Professor Studniczka's identifica-tion of the *Artemis* of Gabii as a copy of this statue, we may see in it a good example of the treatment of an earlier religious conception in the art of the fourth century. It was customary for the women and maidens of Athens, before their marriage and on other occasions, to dedicate a garment to her, and long lists of such

garments are recorded in the inventories of her temple.
The early image of the goddess, an idol of primitive
type, was the centre of this worship, and the garments,
or some of them, were actually placed upon it. In the
*Artemis* of Gabii we see the goddess, clad in the short
and doubly girt chiton of a huntress ; with her two
hands she is employed in fastening with a brooch, on
her right shoulder, a short folded cloak. In this action
we may see a symbolical acceptance by the goddess, for
her own use, of the garments offered by her votaries.
Curiously enough the inscriptions[1] show that the
dedicated garments continued to be placed on the new
statue as they had been on the old one ; and this might
incline us to doubt whether the *Artemis* of Gabii could
be the statue in question. But the doubt is probably
misplaced. Religious conservatism, and the desire of
the worshippers that their offerings should be brought
into actual contact with the goddess, might well over-
ride the artistic respect due to a masterpiece of
Praxiteles. It has also been inferred from the fact that
the old statue is described in the inscription as the
marble one, that the new one by Praxiteles was of
bronze ; and this may well have been the case with the
original of the *Artemis* of Gabii ; it is difficult to judge
of style from a copy, but the clearly cut folds and

---

1 *Cf.* Roberts and Gardner, " Attic Inscriptions," No. 102.

simple modelling would suit bronze technique well
enough ; we certainly do not recognise here the subtlety
in the treatment of marble that distinguishes other
Praxitelean works.  Though the Brauronian *Artemis*
was, in her worship at Athens, an august goddess of
marriage and childbirth, here we find her represented
as the huntress maiden familiar to Greek art.  Such a
rendering is fully in accord with what we should expect
of Praxiteles, who selects the lighter and more graceful
aspect of his subjects ; the delicately symbolic allusion
to the dedication of garments is also in accordance
with his style and with that of the period which he
dominated.

A conjecture made simultaneously by Professor
Benndorf and Professor Furtwängler claimed to add
another to the extant works of Praxiteles.  This is
a head found close to the temple of Hades at Eleusis,
and it was suggested that it represented the Eleusinian
hero Eubuleus, a head of whom, after Praxiteles, was
once set upon a herm of which the shaft only
remained in Rome.  The external evidence for the
identification is not in itself convincing; whether it
should be accepted or not depends entirely on the
style of the head itself.  There is no doubt that in the
treatment of marble and in the delicate finish of surface
it resembles the work of Praxiteles.  The face is of a

youthful but full and rounded type; the small eyes and
somewhat heavy jaw give it an expression at once
melancholy and sensual. Indeed it is difficult to resist
the impression that it is based, at least, on an idealised
portrait rather than on a purely ideal conception of a
mythological character. The luxuriant hair, that frames
the face and shadows the brow, reminds us of that of
the Praxitelean *Satyr*. The shoulders are clad in a light
clinging garment that seems hardly to be finished, and
it is doubtful whether the head was placed upon a
statue or set up on a herm-like shaft. The appropriateness of the type to Eubuleus, the swineherd of Eleusis
who was swallowed up with his herd, and afterwards
became one of the heroes of the mysteries, does not
seem obvious, though the expression of brooding melancholy may suit such a character. Several copies or
replicas of the head have been found both at Eleusis
and elsewhere; it must, therefore, have been a well-
known work. Its meaning must, however, remain somewhat of an enigma; and although its technical qualities
show close affinity to the style of Praxiteles, there seems
no sufficient reason for assigning it to the master himself; it certainly lacks the grace and distinction of touch
that we expect to find in an original from his hand.

Another head claimed by good authorities as an
original by Praxiteles is the head from the Aberdeen

collection now in the British Museum. This is a far more pleasing work, and has the same exquisite finish of surface, the same appearance of life and warmth of modelling which we see in the *Hermes*. The expression is indeed more alert and less dreamy, and there is more indication of physical strength about the Aberdeen head ; these characteristics have led to the suggestion that it represents a young *Heracles*. But in addition to the Praxitelean qualities in the head there are others of a different kind. The whole build of the skull, with its thick-set, compact shape, and above all the form of the brow, is in constrast with the usual Praxitelean proportions and the easy sweep of line from front to side which we usually find in Praxitelean figures. The way in which the brow projects at the sides, and the cushion of flesh swells over it to shadow and almost hide the outer corners of the eyes, reminds us irresistibly of the work of Scopas. There is perhaps nothing impossible in one great sculptor adopting a device which is peculiarly characteristic of his contemporary ; but it is, perhaps, more likely that where we see the qualities of the two combined, as we do here, we should rather assign the work to a colleague or pupil who fell under the influence of both. The head is certainly an original of fourth-century workmanship.

It would be easy to multiply examples of sculpture

that may be attributed to the immediate surroundings
of Praxiteles.  Among these, as being in our own
national museum, may be mentioned the head of
Asclepius from Melos, with its wonderful characterisation of the half-divine, half-human physician, its benign
dignity and thoughtful tranquillity; and the bronze
head of *Sleep*, which may be restored to a statue with
the help of another copy in Madrid.  Here again, in
the graceful figure of the god as he floats over the earth
to pour the balm of sleep for mortals, and in the easy
flow of the modelling, we recognise the influence of
Praxiteles, if not the hand of the master himself.  All
later Greek and Græco-Roman art is full of the grace
and delicacy, of the love of beautiful forms and lines for
their own sake, that were derived above all from him ;
and if the result is sometimes too lacking in vigour and
originality, too ready to sacrifice strength to grace, the
fault of this does not rest with him ; for his own works,
so far as we possess them, never lack the higher qualities
of sculpture, nobility of type, directness of observation,
and distinction in modelling.

The lighter side of his work is also to be seen reflected
in the innumerable statuettes of terra-cotta that have
been found in Greece, and above all those associated
with the name of Tanagra.  These varied studies of
figures, above all female figures, in every variety of

graceful pose and endless change of motive in the
arrangement of their richly flowing drapery, have long
won the admiration of collectors and amateurs, and
seem to bring us into touch with everyday Greek life
in a way impossible to the more imposing masterpieces
of monumental sculpture.  It had long been surmised
that these terra-cotta figurines owed their inspiration
to the Attic school of the fourth century, and above all
to Praxiteles ; and the surmise received strong confirmation when the French excavators discovered at Mantinea
the reliefs that had ornamented the basis of his group
of *Leto and Her Children.*  The subject of these reliefs,
which are referred to by Pausanias, is the musical
contest between Apollo and his lyre and the satyr
Marsyas with the flutes in the presence of the nine
Muses.  The design of the composition, though not its
execution in detail, must probably be assigned to
Praxiteles ; and in his figures of the Muses, seated
or standing in graceful poses and varied arrangements
of drapery, we see a set of figures that may well have
served as prototypes to many of the Tanagra statuettes.
It is not, however, in terra-cottas only that these
Praxitelean Muses find their counterparts.  The tendency, inherited by Greek art from its earliest days, to
repeat a few favourite types with many variations
of detail was continued into the fourth century and

PLATE XLIX

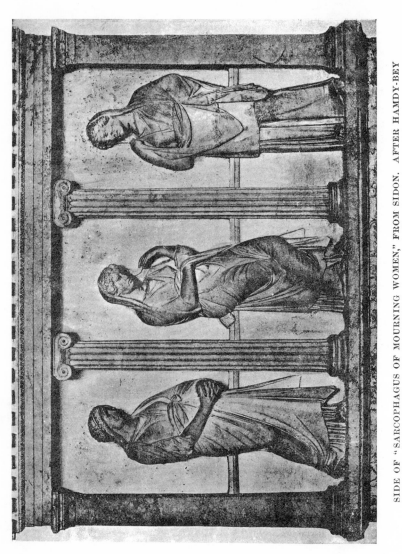

SIDE OF "SARCOPHAGUS OF MOURNING WOMEN," FROM SIDON. AFTER HAMDY-BEY
AND REINACH, *NÉCROPOLE ROYALE À SIDON*, PL. VII

*To face p.* 173

even into Græco-Roman art, in no case more readily
than in these draped figures. We do not know
whether Praxiteles was the first to adapt them to the
representation of the nine Muses; it is probable that
he may here be following his father or elder brother
Cephisodotus, who made a famous group of the *Muses*
on Mount Helicon. Similar figures are also to be seen in
great numbers upon Attic tombstones, and also upon a
monument which clearly owes its inspiration to the same
artistic tendencies, the sarcophagus of a Sidonian prince,
upon each of the four sides of which, set between the
columns of an Ionic temple, we see a series of female
figures in various attitudes of grief. These " mourning
women," from whom the work is generally known as the
*Sarcophage des Pleureuses,* are not too overwhelmed
with their grief to preserve the grace and dignity, the
gentle and restrained pathos which characterise the
graves of the Athenian cemetery. In the careful and
somewhat artificial arrangement of their cloaks, often
enveloping one or both arms, we see a fashion which,
originating in Athens in the fourth century, had a
dominating influence upon later portrait sculpture.
Such sculpture in Athens was especially associated with
tombs, on which it was not uncommon to set up a statue,
not indeed an exact portrait of the deceased, but ideally
commemorative of her. We are informed that works

by Praxiteles were to be seen in the Athenian Ceramicus;
and the reference is very probably to a statue such as
this, set up in the cemetery, perhaps the mourning
lady (*flens matrona*), who reminds us of the title of
the Sidon sarcophagus. It was probably only a
rhetorical device such as pleased the later Greek critics
to contrast it with the "smiling courtesan," doubtless
the portrait of *Phryne*. What such a statue of a
mourning lady could be in the Athenian cemetery of
the fourth century is shown us by the statue from
Trentham recently acquired by the British Museum.
This statue, as its inscription shows, was used again in
Roman times; and late Græco-Roman sculpture frequently repeated the type with variations, for example,
in the two portrait statues from Herculaneum, of which
one is here reproduced. Such statues are sometimes
described as *Roman Lady as a Muse;* but the type
was not restricted to Muses. We see, perhaps, in
the Trentham lady the earliest and finest example,
alike in the delicacy of its execution and the gentle
melancholy of its pose, worthy of the Praxitelean
influence to which we must assign its origin.

It may be noticed that no attempt has here been
made to treat the works of Praxiteles in chronological
order, and so to trace the development of his style. A
good deal has been done in this direction by previous

PLATE L

PORTRAIT OF A LADY, FROM HERCULANEUM,
IN DRESDEN

*To face p.* 174

writers, though their results do not always agree. The external data for fixing the chronological sequence of the various statues are scanty. It has been suggested, for example, that Praxiteles' work at Mantinea was contemporary with that of Cephisodotus at Megalopolis, when, in 370 B.C., the cities of the Peloponnese were reorganised under Epaminondas. It has even been suggested that at this period Praxiteles may have fallen under the influence of the Polyclitan school, which may be seen in the modelling of his *Satyr* as cup-bearer. But it does not seem necessary to look outside Attica for the influences that affected the earlier work of Praxiteles. The *Satyr*, as we have seen, is based to a great extent on an earlier statue of an *Athlete* that is admittedly Attic, whether we assign it to the school of Myron or to Alcamenes. Again, the perfection of technique in the *Hermes* leads us naturally to assign it to the sculptor's maturity; but here we must remember that we have to deal with an original, elsewhere often with copies that may either have lost the character of the original altogether, or have imported into earlier Praxitelean works certain characteristics that the master himself did not adopt until his later period. Where so much dispute is possible it has seemed safer to proceed from what is certain to what is uncertain, to study an original work before turning to copies, and well-attested examples befoie such as can only be attributed to Praxiteles by inference or conjecture.  In whatever order we may study his works, the individuality and artistic character of the master stand out clearly enough.

# CHAPTER VII

## SCOPAS

Scopas is in many ways the most modern of all ancient sculptors; his works give the most direct denial to the often repeated assertion that Greek art lacks individuality and the power to express emotion. We are, indeed, told that Praxiteles also "infused into marble the emotions of the soul," and we have seen to what degree and in what manner we can trace this attainment in his extant works. It consists rather of a study of mood or temperament than of actual emotion, and thus may well escape appreciation, especially where we are dependent upon copies that are sure to miss the subtler qualities of the original. Scopas, on the other hand, is now known to us as the master of passion, whether in the actual energy of strife or feeling, or in the character stamped upon the features by a passionate nature. His wonderful power in this direction cannot be overlooked even by the most casual observer; and it marks him as the originator of that

dramatic tendency in art which is one of the chief
characteristics of the sculpture of the Hellenistic age.
It is for this reason that Scopas naturally comes to
be placed later than Praxiteles in a series of Greek
sculptors.  So far as actual chronology goes, he was
probably the elder of the two.  The dates of his artistic
career, unlike those of Praxiteles, are well attested.
He built the temple of Athena Alea at Tegea, and
also provided it with sculpture, after its destruction
by fire in 395 B.C.  He was also one of the four
sculptors employed on the tomb of Mausolus, who
died either in 353 or 351 B.C., and whose monument,
erected by his wife Artemisia, was not completed until
after her death in 350 B.C.  He made, too, it is said,
one of the sculptured columns of the temple of Artemis
at Ephesus when rebuilt after its destruction by fire in
356 B.C.  His artistic career must therefore be assigned
to the years preceding the middle of the fourth century.
We have no evidence of his undertaking any work later
than 350 B.C., though the completion of the Mausoleum
may have occupied some considerable time.  The
temple at Tegea is generally regarded as his earliest
recorded work ; but the marked individuality of treatment which we see in its sculpture shows that he had
already developed the artistic character that distinguishes him from all other Greek sculptors.  This

individuality is, indeed, so remarkable as to have led
some authorities to assign the work at Tegea to the
period of the Arcadian revival in 370 B.C. It is, perhaps, improbable that they should precede the time of
Scopas' mature activity on the Mausoleum by as much
as forty years, though, in the case of such an artist, an
argument from improbability cannot be pressed; and
his employment as architect is perhaps more likely at
an earlier date.

The temple of Athena Alea at Tegea is described by
Pausanias as easily excelling all others in the Peloponnese, both in size and in beauty of construction and
ornament; it seems to have shown a happy combination of the three orders—Doric and Corinthian without
and Ionic within. In this respect, and also in the
exquisite finish of its architectural mouldings, it resembles the famous Tholos at Epidaurus—the design
of another sculptor, the younger Polyclitus. There is
an interesting coincidence in the almost simultaneous
employment of two sculptors, Scopas and the younger
Polyclitus, on two buildings which Pausanias especially
selects to praise for the beauty of their proportions and
workmanship. And this coincidence is yet more note-
worthy, if we accept the conjecture that the Aristandros
of Paros, who worked at Amyclæ with the elder
Polyclitus on a trophy for the victory of Ægospotami,

was the father of Scopas.[1]  For, if so, we might well infer that the two younger artists were brought up in the common tradition of the Argive school—as is attested for Polyclitus, and probable, as we shall see, for Scopas also.

The sculptures of the temple at Tegea are described by Pausanias as follows: "The pedimental group in the front is the hunt of the Calydonian boar; the boar is almost exactly in the centre of the composition; on the one side of it are Atalanta, Meleager, and Theseus, Telamon, Peleus, Polydeuces, and Iolaus, who helped Heracles in most of his labours, and the sons of Thestius and brothers of Althæa, Prothous and Cometes.  On the other side of the boar is Ancæus, who is now wounded and has dropped his axe, supported by Epiochus; beside him is Castor and Amphiaraus the son of Oicleus; beyond them Hippothous the son of Cercyon the son of Agamedes the son of Stymphalus; and last of all is represented Pirithous.  In the pediment at the back is the battle of Telephus against Achilles in the plain of the Caïcus. . . . Beside the statue of *Athena* (within the temple) stand on the one side *Asclepius*, on the other *Hygieia*, of Pentelic marble,

1 The conjecture rests on the fact that the names Scopas and Aristandros occur in alternating generations in a Parian family of sculptors of later date.

the work of Scopas of Paros." The subjects of the pedimental groups are closely associated with the traditions of the temple; within it was preserved the skin of the Calydonian boar, dedicated, it was said, by Atalanta herself when it had been awarded to her for her valour in saving Ancæus and being the first to wound the monster. Telephus also, who led an Arcadian colony to Mysia, was said to have been the child of Auge, the priestess of Athena Alea, and of Heracles, who had met her near the temple, and who subsequently recognised his son being suckled by a doe on the neighbouring Mount Parthenium; Telephus and his followers fought against the Greeks who landed near Pergamus on their way to Troy; a romantic feature in the story—a favourite theme in later drama and art—was the tale of how the wound that Achilles had given Telephus could only be healed by the hand of him who had inflicted it. It is not easy to see how this could have been introduced even by implication into the scene of combat, but it can hardly be doubted that Scopas made the most of the pathetic interest of the story. Here, unfortunately, Pausanias' brief reference does not help us; but the composition of the other pediment can be reconstructed from his description. The central group was evidently formed by Atalanta, Meleager, Theseus, and the boar; this

central group was bounded on each side by a hero
supporting a wounded comrade; for we learn from other
sources that Telamon was said to have stumbled, and
to have been rescued by Peleus. It is evident that the
two Dioscuri, Castor and Polydeuces, balance each other
on the two sides of the group; it is useless to conjecture the position of the remaining figures; but the
strictly symmetrical composition is sufficiently indicated by the description to justify the following
scheme—

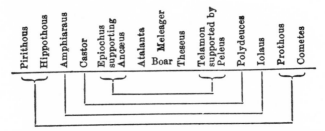

It will be better to reserve any further discussion of
this pediment until we have noticed the extant remains
of the sculpture found at Tegea. Some of these, which
have been known for a considerable time, are the boar's
head and two heads of heroes, one helmeted and one
bare, together with some other fragments of limbs.
The more recent excavations, by M. Mendel, of the
French school at Athens, have added two more heads
of warriors, one of them covered with a lion's scalp,

PLATE LI

HEAD OF HERACLES, FROM TEGEA, BY SCOPAS.  AFTER *BULLETIN DE CORR. HELIÉNIQUE*, 1901, VII

*To face p. 183*

after the custom of Heracles, and some portions of
other figures and of dogs. All these are in the marble
from the local quarries of Doliana. Other portions of
figures found in the recent excavations are in Parian
marble; among these are a torso of a female figure in
Amazonian dress, and a head on the same scale, and
very probably belonging to this torso. It is probable
that all these fragments come from the pediments of
the temple; the torso, indeed, can hardly represent
any other figure than Atalanta herself. The difference
of material is the only difficulty; but this may be
explained by the fact that the Parian marble belongs to
the only female figure—so far as we know—in the two
groups. For a sculptor might well prefer to use the
finer material to render the face and arms and legs of
the heroine; they would be left, as was usual in Greek
sculpture, in the natural colour of the marble, while the
male figures would probably be more or less coloured,
especially in architectural work. A striking analogy
is to be seen in the *Demeter* of Cnidus; there the
sculptor, content with an inferior local marble for the
drapery, has chosen Parian marble as allowing the finer
surface and finish he required in the head of the
goddess.

The boar and the dogs must come from the east
pediment, and it can hardly be doubted that the female

torso is that of the huntress Atalanta from the same pediment.  It is impossible to distribute the rest of the fragments with any certainty between the two pediments, though it may be suggested that the helmeted heads are more likely to belong to the battle scene, the bare heads to the hunt.  *Heracles* is a difficulty in either case; for he was not in the group of the boar-hunt; nor is his presence—especially as a combatant— to be expected in the fight between his son Telephus and Achilles.  Possibly some other hero may here have borrowed his attribute of the lion's scalp— perhaps Telephus himself.  All the heads alike—with the exception of the one that may be assigned to Atalanta—are marked by an intensity of expression that may find its motive in the stress either of the battle or of the hunt.  It is, indeed, this intensity of expression that is the chief characteristic of the Tegean sculptures, and that distinguishes them from all earlier work.  It is the more remarkable from the early date to which the pediments must probably be assigned; we may justly infer that Scopas seems early in his career to have formed the style which seems to have so great and lasting an influence.  The means by which this expression is attained are mainly the direction of the gaze and the deep overshadowing of the eye; these are enhanced by the choice of a massive physical type which lends itself to strength and passion rather than to the lighter emotions, and which, at the same time, tends to confirm the conjecture that the training of Scopas was obtained in the Argive rather than in the Attic school. It is above all the modelling of the flesh around the eye that is characteristic; a heavy roll of it, curving out from beneath the brow, overshadows the outer corner of the eye, so that the upper eyelid is actually embedded in it. The impression of the eye being fixed on the distance is produced by a wide opening of the eyelids, which also shortens the eye from side to side. This, with the dilated nostril, and the half-open, panting mouth, in which the teeth are clearly visible, gives a feeling of strain and intensity to the faces such as is hardly to be matched in any other work of ancient sculpture. The subjects of the two pediments, in the one case a conflict in which intensity of passion was succeeded by a pathetic and even dramatic situation, in the other a combat with a terrible monster, and a combat that ended in a tragic rivalry, involving the death of several of the principal participants, were such as to justify the intense and passionate expression of the faces.

So far all the characters represented have been spoken of together, and, in the absence of certain criteria for identification, there seems no need to draw any distinc-

tion between them ; a description applying to one
would also, in all essential matters, apply to all, though
they differ in accessories and in degree of preservation.
Even in the heads of the beasts, the boar and the dogs,
we find the same trick, as we may almost call it, of the
heavy roll of flesh overshadowing the eye.    But in the
one female head, if it be rightly joined to the torso and
identified as *Atalanta*, we find a great contrast in this
respect.    Though her face is full of life, expressed in
the mobility of the lips and the soft rendering of the
flesh between brow and eyelid, it shows a remarkable
absence of the intensity which marks the expression
of the other faces.    Some authorities would therefore
deny the attribution of this head to the pediments ;
but the difference may be explained by the intention of
the sculptor to contrast the serenity of the heroine,
who is something more than human, with the human
passions of the heroes who surround her.    The face
shows by no means a commonplace type of the early
fourth century, but is worthy of a sculptor noted for
his originality.    If in this case he has not thrown the
eyes into deep shadow, we must remember that such
a device was comparatively new, and that it was still
in the experimental stage ; it was natural enough that,
wanting a contrast, he should apply the new method
only to the male heads and not to the *Atalanta*, though

female heads made later by him or under his influence show something of the same intensity of gaze, expressed by similar modelling.

The torso of *Atalanta* is also valuable as giving us for the first time a clear example of Scopas' treatment of drapery. Its arrangement, of studied simplicity yet aiming at and attaining a strong effect, and the detail of its execution, its broader contours varied by smaller realistic touches in detail, are characteristic of the master. It is to be seen not only in copies of statues directly assignable to Scopas, such as the *Mœnad*, but also in many other fourth-century and later works that show his influence—notably the *Amazons* of the Mausoleum frieze, the statues of *Mausolus* and *Artemisia*, and the *Demeter* of Cnidus.

Besides the Tegean pediments, we have in the sculpture of the Mausoleum another example of extant works assigned by ancient authorities to Scopas. But in this case the question is complicated by the mention of three other sculptors associated with him; and it seems better to reserve these sculptures until we can obtain some further criteria as to his style from other works which, if only as later copies, may be attributed to him on external evidence. Here, however, we must remember that the extraordinary originality and subtlety of Scopas' work was certain to suffer greatly at the hand

of a copyist, and lose so much of his personal touch as
to degenerate on the one hand into exaggeration, on
the other into the comparatively commonplace.  For
this reason we shall find contemporary sculptures, even
if they can only be assigned to his associates or pupils,
more satisfactory in many ways than later copies ; and
we must, therefore, recur to them in any attempt to
estimate the work of Scopas as a whole.

Among the recorded works of Scopas none is perhaps
so characteristic as his *Mœnad*.   Such a subject, representing the bacchic frenzy in its most ecstatic form,
might well seem at first sight beyond the bounds
that Greek sculpture usually set itself; epigrams and
rhetorical descriptions emulate one another in testifying
to the life of the work.   The *Mœnad*, in her inspired
madness, had slain a fawn, and she carried its lifeless
body in her hand.   Descriptions of such a statue would
be of little use to us, if they had not led to the
identification of a statuette in Dresden [1] as a copy of
it.  Here we see the *Mœnad* advancing in a kind
of rhythmic motion that serves to counterbalance the
unbridled wildness of her passion.   Her head is thrown
back so that the face is almost horizontal, her hair is
unbound, and the drapery, still fastened on her
shoulders and held together by her girdle, floats open

[1] Published by Professor Treu in " Mélanges Perrot."

PLATE LII

MÆNAD, AFTER SCOPA.   AFTER *MÉLANGES*
PERROT, PL. V

*To face p.* 188

below so as to leave bare her left leg and the left side
of her body. On her left shoulder are traces showing
where she had slung the dead body of her victim; her
right hand, lowered, doubtless held the knife or sword.
Even in a copy of Roman date and on a small scale—
about two-fifths of life—it is possible to appreciate the
firm beauty of the youthful figure, the skill with which
the broad folds of the drapery are enlivened, as in the
*Atalanta,* by realistic touches of detail, above all the
composition, which transforms what in some hands
might be a painful or even a brutal subject into an
impersonation of orgiastic enthusiasm. The subject
was not a new one in the time of Scopas; even the
dancing step and the head thrown back are to be found
in Attic works of the fifth century, which have themselves a certain affected grace and refinement, qualities
that were exaggerated into a mannerism by later
imitators. Scopas has, without sacrificing the beauty
of the type, filled it with life and reality. When we
come to consider details, we find this *Mœnad* in every
way characteristic of the master. This is above all the
case with the face; in its damaged condition, the character of the expression is obscured, and, even apart from
this, it had probably suffered much at the hands of the
copyist. Yet we can recognise in it the same intensity
of expression that we see in the Tegea heads, the same

roll of flesh overshadowing the eyes and even em-
bedding the upper eyelid.   Here then Scopas must
have followed, in the rendering of a woman's head, the
same means of expressing passion which he used in the
male heads at Tegea.

With the help of this head we may identify, as
showing very strongly the influence of Scopas, some
other female heads that have survived from the fourth
century.   Closest of all these to his style, as we have
come to recognise it, is a head from Laurium which,
partly owing to its discoloration from being submerged in the sea amidst the refuse of the Laurium
mines, has not hitherto met with the appreciation
which it deserves.[1]   This head is clearly that of a
goddess, probably Aphrodite, drawing together with
one hand on the top of her head the long tresses into
which her hair has been plaited, perhaps for the bath.
The hair and hand are only roughly finished, but the
face lacks nothing of perfection in workmanship.   In it
we see again the full, rounded proportions, the intense,
far-away gaze, the distended nostril, the half-open lips,
and all the other indications which we have learnt to
regard as Scopas' favourite expressions of a passionate

1 Published by E. F. Benson in the " Journal of Hellenic Studies,"
xv. p. 194.   He rightly rejects the old interpretation as *Apollo
Lyceus.*

nature. Above all, there is a warmth of life such as is to be seen in only a few of the heads that have survived from ancient times. Various statues of *Aphrodite* by Scopas are recorded, one of them later in Rome, in which he is said to have rivalled Praxiteles himself in his rendering of the goddess nude. The motive of the bath, evidently present in this statue as in the Cnidian *Aphrodite*, suggests the comparison; and, if it is justified, we seem to have in this head some kind of contemporary replica of Scopas' work. Another head of a goddess that has often been quoted as showing resemblance to the style of Scopas is the one found to the south of the Acropolis in Athens.[1] This seems to have been a well-known work, as there is a copy of it— or of its original—in Berlin. Though it has not quite the same correspondence in details to the Tegea heads that we see in the Laurium head, it shows a good deal of the same character, in the simple and massive forms, the parted lips and dilated nostrils, and in the wide-open and deeply shadowed eyes. The hair, with its crisp and rippled texture, is in contrast with the soft Praxitelean treatment of female hair, but resembles what we see in the *Demeter* of Cnidus, another work that must certainly be placed in the same category, even if its relation to Scopas himself be not closer.

1 Handbook, Fig. 101.

This statue of *Demeter*, originally set up in the
precinct of the Gods of the Lower World at Cnidus, is
in many ways interesting.   It was not, indeed, a temple
statue in the narrower sense, but in all probability a
dedication.   But there can be no doubt that it is an
original work of about the middle of the fourth century
B.C.   We are told that Cnidus possessed many marble
statues by famous masters, among them some by
Scopas; and the fact that others were by Praxiteles
and Bryaxis suggests that the Cnidans took advantage of
the presence of these famous sculptors at Halicarnassus,
just across the gulf, where the *Mausoleum* was being
built under their direction, and were thus enabled to
enrich the shrines of Cnidus with works of the most distinguished masters of fourth-century art.   The *Demeter*
evidently belongs to this time and to this set of statues.
Perhaps a more careful examination will justify us in
going even further.   The statue is the one selected by
Brunn in his " Griechische Götterideale " to illustrate
and to justify his criticism of the common assumption
that, " while Greek art is supreme in beauty of form, it
is surpassed by Christian art in depth of expression."
Its subject lends itself to such comparison, since it
offers an expression of sorrow such as is alien to a great
deal of what is most characteristic of Greek art.
When, however, we have, as in this case, a deviation

PLATE LIII

HEAD OF DEMETER OF CNIDUS, IN BRITISH MUSEUM

*To face p.* 192

from the healthy and normal type, it is instructive to
notice in what the deviation consists.   Here we see
the impersonation of the mother mourning the loss of
her child ; and the beauty of the form and the subtlety
with which the sorrow is expressed may serve at first
sight to conceal the intensity of the expression.  But
the power is there, and if the effect seems mild in
comparison with the emaciated and ascetic forms and
the distortion of feature which we sometimes see in
Christian art—and, it may be added, in some products
of Hellenistic art—yet the very restraint which the
artist's sense of sculptural fitness has imposed upon
him should really increase our appreciation of his
work.  For, when we study the face closely, there is
even emaciation to be found in the wasted tissues
around the eye-socket, and in the slightly hollow
cheeks ; but it is rendered with such restraint and refinement that we are hardly conscious of it, although the
impression it produces is not for that reason lost ; and
when we compare the head of this sorrowing mother
with the passionate goddess that we have recognised in
the Laurium head, the contrast is striking.  But, for
all this contrast, the two have much in common—a
similar physical type, the same far-away look in the
eyes, though here directed not upwards, but on the
distant horizon, the same treatment of nostrils and

N

mouth.   There is, above all, in both alike that warmth
of life which we only see in a few originals of fourth-
century date, and which is absent both from the
severer work of an earlier age and from the conventional
or exaggerated efforts of the Hellenistic period.   A
curious thing about this Cnidian *Demeter* is that the
sculptor, in order to do justice to his modelling of the
face, has made the head of Parian marble, though he
has contented himself, for the body and the drapery,
with an inferior local marble which will not take or
preserve so fine a surface.   Here we are reminded of
the *Atalanta* of Tegea among the other pedimental
figures of local marble ; and the reason for the choice
is probably in both cases the same.   The treatment of
the drapery is also characteristic ; it is drawn across
and across the body in a somewhat restless manner,
very different from the harmonious and simple folds
which we usually find in Praxitelean works ; there is,
however, no confusion, and the realistic touches that
give life to the folds do not obscure their general
arrangement.   There is in this the germ of that somewhat exaggerated treatment of drapery for effect that
we find in many works of the Hellenistic age ; but here
the drapery as well as the face shows the restraint
characteristic of a fourth-century master.   All this is
what we should expect of Scopas, and although the

attribution of the statue to his hand is, perhaps, beyond the legitimate limits of artistic criticism, there can be no doubt that it is full of his spirit, and made by one of his contemporaries and associates, if not by himself.

Another statue that has survived to our time in several copies, if we do not possess the original, is that of a hero whose tragic and untimely end gives a peculiar interest to his personality; this is the *Meleager* (*see* Pl. I.), which is well known from the Vatican statue; much finer and more accurate copies of this head can be seen on a statue (to which it does not belong) in the Medici gardens, and in the head recently acquired from the Carlisle collection at Castle Howard by the British Museum. A fine though much-damaged copy of the statue exists at Boston. The remains of the short hunting-spear and the boar's head in the Vatican copy show the identification of the ideal hunter to be correct. A comparison between the Vatican and Medici heads, as facilitated by the reproductions on Pl. I. from the Berlin "Antike Denkmäler," I. Pl. XL., is most instructive, for it allows us to compare an ordinary Roman copy of a fourth-century head with what, if not, as some suggest, the original itself, at least preserves much of the chararacter and quality of the original. A glance at this plate tells more than pages of description. The individuality, the life. and the mobility of feature so conspicuous in the one are entirely lost in the other. And this is evidently not due merely to the inability of the later copyist to reproduce what he saw before him. The conventional treatment and vacancy of expression which we see in the later copy are clearly intentional. The sculptor who made the Vatican *Meleager* evidently thought that the expression of a passionate nature, the warmth of life, and the individuality of character shown by such a face as that of the Medici *Meleager* was unsuited to the severe dignity of classical art, and so has substituted for these a more generalised type, comparatively empty of meaning. When we realise that a large number of the copies on which we are dependent for our knowledge of Greek originals were made under conditions similar to those of the Vatican *Meleager*, we see how much allowance it is necessary to make in quoting these copies as evidence for the masters of Greek sculpture. And this is more particularly the case with the sculpture of the fourth century. In the case of earlier work, the copyist, if he failed, as he often did, in preserving the beauty and dignity of his original, failed from lack of power rather than from intention. In reproduction of Hellenistic work, on the other hand, its comparative crudity and exaggeration saved it from the possibility of being refined away by an academic imitator. It is the very subtlety and delicacy with

PLATE LIV

"ARES LUDOVISI"

Between pp. 196 and 197

PLATE LV

HEAD OF "ARES LUDOVISI"

*To face p.* 197

which so much expression is given by the masters of the
fourth century that make copies of their work so often
into mere travesties; it is fortunate that we possess
some contemporary originals or replicas by which the
copies can be tested.

Other statues might easily be quoted in illustration
of the style of Scopas. Among these is the *Ares
Ludovisi*, itself a copy of Roman date, and showing in
its accessories, especially in the baby Cupid playing
between the feet of the god, the taste of a later age.
But the original almost certainly goes back to the time
of Scopas, and the type of face has much resemblance
to the *Meleager*. The manner in which the god is
seated, with one knee drawn up and his hands clasped
about it, evidently shows the difficult self-restraint of a
passionate nature, and is appropriate both to Scopas as
a sculptor and to the war-god as a subject. But the
device is not a new one, and occurs, for example, in the
*Ares* of the Parthenon frieze. Though Scopas made a
colossal seated statue of *Ares*, which was carried off to
Rome in the second century B.C., there is no sufficient
reason to identify the Ludovisi statue as a reduced copy
of this; but he or his associates may well have produced other variations on the type. The face alone
suffices to show that the statue was made under his
influence.

Many other extant statues show the direct influence of Scopas, from unambitious works such as
Attic tombstones to statues such as the Lansdowne
*Heracles.* But in this last example, and in some others,
the case is complicated by another resemblance;
for the style of Lysippus, as revealed to us by the
statue of *Agias*, has much in common with that of
Scopas, and seems to be combined with it in some
instances.[1] The question of the influence of Scopas on
Lysippus must be considered when we are dealing with
the later artist. But in any general estimate of the
work of Scopas this element can scarcely be overlooked,
for through it came an incalculable accession to the
predominance of Scopas over the more vigorous branches
of Hellenistic art. The resemblance of the head of the
Lansdowne *Heracles* to the Tegea heads has led to
a general acceptance of the view that it should be
attributed directly or indirectly to Scopas. It is not
indeed an original, but a copy; and the character of the
expression has been somewhat conventionalised, and the
freshness of the modelling smoothed away, though not
so much so as in the *Meleager* of the Vatican ; we can
easily imagine that the original may have been less
heavy and more vigorous. In the massive build of head,
the deep eye-sockets with their curve of flesh over-

[1] *See* P. Gardner in "Journal of Hellenic Studies," xxiii. p. 128.

PLATE LVI

HERACLES, IN LANSDOWNE HOUSE

*To face p.* 198

PLATE LVII

HEAD OF LANSDOWNE HERACLES

*Between pp.* 198 *and* 199

PLATE LVIII

HEAD OF LANSDOWNE HERACLES

To face p. 139

shadowing and enveloping the outer corner of the eye, in the broad nose and half-open lips, we can recognise all the characteristics that we have learnt to look for in the work of Scopas. The body, too, has the massive type, with the muscles clearly mapped out, that we find in the work of Polyclitus, and so confirms the dependence of Scopas upon the Argive school of athletic art. It is in the proportions of body and limbs, as well as of the head, that we see the contrast with the lighter and more agile Lysippean type which we see in the *Agias* —a contrast too essential to be explained by the fact that heavier proportions are suitable to the type of *Heracles*, and emphasised the more by the similarity in position of the two statues. This position is a variation on the rigid walking pose which we see in the *Dory-phorus* of Polyclitus, which, in the similarity of the position of the arms and upper part of the torso, the Lansdowne *Heracles* again recalls. The weight is more evenly divided between the two feet, and the thigh is swung out further to the side, giving greater elasticity of appearance. In the Lansdowne *Heracles* we see, indeed, an intermediate stage between the style of Polyclitus and that of Lysippus, and this accords well with its attribution to Scopas.

A happy application of literary evidence to the identification of extant works concerns a series of

representations which Brunn, with his intuitive criticism, was able to recognise as characteristic of Scopas,
and even to make the basis of many inferences as to the
master's style which have since been confirmed by the
discovery of the Tegean heads. Noting that Pliny
quotes as of the highest estimation among the works of
Scopas a group of sea creatures, Posidon and Thetis
and Achilles, with Nereids on sea monsters and Tritons,
he observed that many sculptures of this and similar
subjects existed in museums. Many of these are merely
decorative works of later style; but among them are a
few which show a distinctive character, and suggest
association with a sculptor who could express the soul
through the features. In the heads of a *Triton* and
other similiar works, Brunn saw a vivid impersonation
of the genius of the sea, wayward and passionate, ever
longing for the earth and its creatures, yet never
pacified, its readiness to receive every impulse typified
by the mobile features. In these semi-human forms
we may see a wilder and more unbridled passion than in
the heroes of Tegea, or even in the *Mœnad*. We
have, indeed, no such evidence as would justify us in
regarding any of these representations of Tritons or
other inhabitants of the sea as direct copies from the
work of Scopas; but when we consider both their
artistic character and the nature of the influence which

he exercised, we can hardly doubt that his treatment of
the subject must have dominated all later imitators.
It is instructive to compare this predilection of Scopas
for the wild creatures of the sea, their passionate long-
ings and intense eagerness, with the happy and passive
nature given by Praxiteles to his *Satyr*, the wild
creature of the woods. In this comparison is summarised the whole contrast between the two sculptors.

So far we have not considered the Mausoleum, which
may seem in many ways to offer the most satisfactory
evidence as to Scopas, since he is known to have been
employed upon it, and a considerable amount of the
sculpture with which it was decorated has been recovered, and is now in the British Museum. The
difficulty of using this evidence lies in the fact that
Scopas was not the only sculptor employed. We have,
indeed, a most circumstantial statement by Pliny that
Scopas undertook the sculpture on the east, Bryaxis on
the north, Timotheus on the south, and Leochares on
the west. Whether we accept this version of the story
as probable or not—and there are rival traditions
which bring in Praxiteles—there can be little doubt
that the sculpture of the Mausoleum was produced by
the co-operation of four or five of the most famous
sculptors of the middle of the fourth century, with
Scopas at their head. A book was written about the

Mausoleum by its architects, and with such an authority
before them, the later compilers can hardly be entirely
wrong.   At the same time, the variations that occur
seem to show that this treatise, which probably was
written mainly, if not entirely, from the architectural
point of view, was not very explicit about the distribution of the sculptural work.   With the architectural
restoration of the building, a problem that has exercised
and still exercises the ingenuity of architects, we are
only concerned here so far as it affects the position of
the sculpture.   Though there are numerous divergencies
of opinion as to details, it is generally agreed that the
Mausoleum was more or less in the shape of a temple,
surrounded by columns, supported on a lofty basis, and
carrying above it a pyramid that formed a pedestal for
the colossal chariot that crowned the whole structure.
The more important portions of the sculpture that have
been recovered consist of the remains of three friezes,
and of several statues in the round, some of which may
very probably have been placed in the two pediments
of the temple-like portion of the monument.   How all
the friezes were placed is a disputed question, for the
decision of which there is no sufficient evidence ; what
concerns us most at present is to know whether they
went round all four sides of the building ; for in that
case they would, if the literary tradition be taken

literally, have to be distributed, each of them, among
the four sculptors concerned. The analogy of the
*Nereid* monument in the British Museum and of the
Sarcophagus with the mourning women from Sidon [1]
may give us a very fair notion of how the sculpture on
such a monument, in the form of an Ionic temple, is likely
to be arranged. In both of these there are pediments
on the two narrower sides; and M. Six's suggestion [2]
that the eastern pediment of the Mausoleum was
occupied by enthroned figures and a scene of sacrifice,
and the western by a hunting scene, is quite in accordance with analogy. If so, these two would doubtless
be by Scopas and Leochares respectively. Leochares,
in conjunction with Lysippus, made a similar hunting
scene in commemoration of a monarch's exploits in
Alexander's lion-hunt at Delphi; to this western pediment the splendid figure of a prancing horse with a
rider in Oriental dress would belong. The enthroned
figures would be the work of Scopas; these doubtless,
on the analogy of the *Nereid* monument, represented
the heroised pair, Mausolus and Artemisia. The
seated male figure from the Mausoleum has sometimes
been called Zeus; but the high boot is more appropriate to Mausolus. The absence of finish at the back
suits a pedimental figure. In its mutilated condition it

[1] *See* p. 173.          [2] J. H. S., xxv. p. 1.

is difficult to form any very clear notion of its artistic
character; but the treatment of the drapery is again
similar to what we saw in the *Atalanta*. The colossal
female head, which probably belongs to the figure of
Artemisia in this same pediment, loses something of its
effect from the conventional head-dress of three rows
of spiral curls—doubtless a local Court fashion. But in
the massive proportions and simplicity of modelling, in
the wide-open eyes, overshadowed by the flesh beneath
the brow, in the dilated nostrils and half-open lips, we
have all the characteristics which we noticed in the
Tegea heads here transferred to an ideal portrait; and
in the expression, recalling that of the Cnidian *Demeter*,
it is hardly rash to see a reminiscence of the wifely
mourning which expressed itself in so splendid a
monument. It is unfortunate that the face of the
standing statue of *Artemisia*—not, presumably, by
Scopas—is not preserved for comparison. In considering the authorship of the friezes of the Mausoleum,
the recorded distribution of the sides among the
different sculptors is of little use to us. So far as can
be ascertained, the various friezes must probably have
run all round the building. It is therefore impossible
to say which slabs belong to which side. An attempt
to do this on the ground of style was disproved by
technical indications in the thickness or finish of the

PLATE LIX

HEAD, PROBABLY OF ARTEMISIA, FROM MAUSOLEUM

*To face p.* 204

PLATE LX

CHARIOTEER, FROM FRIEZE OF MAUSOLEUM

To fac p. 205

slabs; but on the other hand these technical indications do not suffice for any systematic division of the slabs between the sides. This is the less to be regretted since, whatever division between the different masters may have been possible in the case of pedimental groups and other sculptures, in the case of a continuous frieze round the building it is not easy to imagine that it was independently designed by four different men. More probably each frieze was designed as a whole by one of the sculptors, the execution being carried out by assistants under his supervision, and very likely completed in detail by the master's own hand. There are only two friezes well enough preserved to be of much value from the artistic point of view; and of one of these, the frieze of racing chariots, there is only one figure left in anything like a complete state. But this one figure is, perhaps, the most characteristic of all that we have of the sculpture of the Mausoleum; it shows us the ideal charioteer, with eager eyes and parted lips, his hair and drapery streaming in the wind, the whole with a warmth of life and passion such as it is difficult to assign to any other master than Scopas himself. If it is not by him, then it testifies to the marvellous degree in which he had imparted his own spirit and his own skill in execution to those who were his associates in the decoration of the Mausoleum.

Of the other frieze, representing the combat of
Greeks and Amazons, far more is left, so that we can
obtain a very fair notion of the composition of the whole.
Here again, on external evidence, the authorship of
Scopas has not a high degree of probability ; and if we
see in it many touches that recall his work elsewhere,
the inference must be that his influence dominated his
companions, rather than that he designed the whóle
himself.   Even if there were no literary record connecting Scopas with the Mausoleum, there are so many
points of resemblance between the frieze and his extant
works that it must inevitably have been associated with
him.   There is a tense eagerness about the position
and expression of the various figures which recalls the
Tegea heads, and a continuous rhythm harmonising the
violence of action, as in the *Mœnad.*   There are many
details, too, which resemble the work of Scopas—for
instance, the way in which the garments of the
Amazons often float open, held in only by the girdle,
and display the beauty of their form, as in the *Mœnad.*
The way, too, in which each individual figure stands
out by itself must have been found in the Tegea
pediments, where there were only fifteen [1] combatants
to fill the field of the gable of a large temple.   The

[1] In the Parthenon there are twenty-two figures in each pediment, at Olympia twenty-one.

PLATE LXI

To face p. 206

FRIEZE OF MAUSOLEUM; BATTLE OF GREEKS AND AMAZONS

PLATE LXII

FRIEZE OF MAUSOLEUM; BATTLE OF GREEKS AND AMAZONS

*Between pp. 206 and 207*

PLATE LXIII

FRIEZE OF MAUSOLEUM; BATTLE OF GREEKS AND AMAZONS

*Between pp. 206 and 207*

PLATE LXIV

APOLLO, FROM MAUSOLEUM

*To face p.* 207

slender proportions of the figures, as well as some other
characteristics in the work, must rather be due to the
Attic collaborators of Scopas; but the whole spirit of
the frieze, with its dramatic and impetuous vigour, its
touches of pathos and of passion, shows how much they
owed to his inspiration.

Among the various statues found in or near the
Mausoleum, and therefore presumably to be assigned
to one or other of its sculptors, is a head and probably
the draped shoulders also of an *Apollo*. There is
again no external evidence to show to which of the
sculptors this head should be assigned; and if we can
see in it many resemblances to the work of Scopas, this
does not preclude the possibility of its being made by
one of the others who were under his influence. Both
Leochares and Bryaxis must have been quite young
men at the time; while Timotheus, the representative
of the older Attic tradition, is evidently out of question.
The type is clearly that of the impassioned musician,
his eyes upraised as if to seek inspiration; the massive
build of the head, and the heavy over-shadowing of the
eyes at the side, remind us of the work of Scopas, and
the resultant expression has again the intensity we
usually find in them; the high and rather narrow forehead, projecting strongly in the middle, is characteristic
of the god rather than of the sculptor; but it is the

type of the god which we find in later fourth-century and Hellenistic art, and which we here find in its earliest extant example, possibly in its original occurrence.   Other statues of *Apollo* are recorded by Scopas among them that of the Palatine *Apollo*, which is probably represented by the *Apollo Citharœdus* of the Vatican.   This represents the god as the inspired musician, advancing in flowing robes as he sings to the lyre, his head raised and his lips half open.   The head from the Mausoleum is by no means similar to the head on the Vatican statue; but we have there to do with a Roman copy, here with a Greek original of the fourth century, and we have seen in the case of the *Meleager* what a difference this may imply.   Even if the *Apollo* of the Mausoleum be not assigned to Scopas himself, it interests us as the prototype of many later representations of the god.

Finally, we may notice an example of the way in which the influence of Scopas had, even in the fourth century, filtered down to such everyday works as the tombstones of Athens.   On one of these we see an athlete whose massive proportions, square brow and deep-set eyes suggest the influence of Scopas, and facing him is an old man whose expression of sorrow shows, once more, the intensity of emotion the great sculptor had taught even the makers of these reliefs to express;

PLATE LXV

STELE FROM THE ILISSUS AT ATHENS

*To face p.* 208

the little boy huddled up at the feet of the athlete
shows a new touch of pathos, keener than the gentle
melancholy that pervades many of these monuments.
We shall have occasion to see how the dramatic and
passionate qualities imported into Greek sculpture by
Scopas pervade the later art of Greece ; here we see an
example of the way in which even the private and
personal emotion of his contemporaries found fuller
expression owing to his influence.

# CHAPTER VIII

## LYSIPPUS

IF our information as to Scopas has been considerably supplemented by recent discoveries, in the case of Lysippus the new evidence has been revolutionary in its character. Hitherto we have been dependent for our estimate of Lysippus upon literary notices of his style and attainments, upon some rather remote copies or imitations of his well-known works, and on one statue, the *Apoxyomenos* of the Vatican, which has generally been regarded as a direct copy of the *Apoxyomenos* made by Lysippus, and has, therefore, been made the basis of all discussion of his style and of the type which he affected. It is true that the weakness of the evidence on which this identification rests was recognised by some critics. But it has generally been held that the extant statue accorded so well with the description of ancient writers as to justify not only its attribution to Lysippus, but its being given the foremost place among his works. Such a view, based merely on probabilities, is clearly

untenable if it be confronted with any positive evidence
that is inconsistent with it. In the French excavations
at Delphi a statue has been found which, as we shall see,
has good claims to be considered as representative of
the work of Lysippus. This statue is quite unlike the
*Apoxyomenos* of the Vatican, and has a strong resemblance to a recognised series of statues, with clearly
marked characteristics, which have hitherto been
generally regarded as showing the influence of Scopas.
It therefore becomes necessary to reconsider our
estimate of the work and character of Lysippus in the
light of this new discovery; and the result will, I think,
be found not only to be more consistent with our
present notion of the development of sculpture in the
fourth century, but also to give us a clearer and more
consistent notion of the master himself. The literary
evidence represents Lysippus as the sculptor who stands
between two epochs, the Hellenic and the Hellenistic.
On the one hand he is, according to our records, the
last of the great masters of Greek sculpture who lived
and worked in Greece itself, and who carried to their
full development the tendencies and traditions of the
Hellenic schools; on the other, he is the man to whom
all the chief schools of the Hellenistic age look back as
to their acknowledged master, and his pupils appear
to have originated many of the most characteristic

developments of Greek art in the East.   He was a Sicyonian by birth, and was the head of the school of Sicyon, to which town the immediate successors of Polyclitus had transferred the school of sculptors which had, under him as under Agelades, had its centre in Argos.   Lysippus thus came to be regarded as the successor of Polyclitus in the theory and practice of athletic art.   Like Polyclitus, he made many statues of Olympian and other victors, and he is also said to have made a special study of athletic proportions, though it is not recorded that he wrote, like his predecessor, a treatise on the subject.   The supposition that he embodied his theory in a statue is based mainly on the analogy of the famous *Doryphorus* of Polyclitus, though it is to some extent justified by the prominent position among his works given by Pliny to the *Apoxyomenos*.   It certainly seems, like the *Doryphorus*, to have been the embodiment of an athletic type or ideal rather than the statue of an individual athlete ; but its importance to our present study to a great extent disappears, now that we cannot with any probability assume that we possess an accurate copy of it.   Lysippus is said to have modified the proportions of the Polyclitan type by making the body more slender, the head smaller, the muscles drier and more sinewy ; and so to have increased the apparent height of the figure.   This

was no sudden innovation; other artists between
Polyclitus and Lysippus had made a study of proportions, notably Euphranor, who is said to have so far
exaggerated the slimness of the limbs as to make the
joints stand out; and the general tendency in the
fourth century was towards lighter and more graceful
forms. The source of our information about Lysippus
is probably to be sought in a criticism emanating from
his school, and regarding him as the last of the great
masters; in describing his peculiar attainments, it
sums up the development of a century. But we need
not, therefore, doubt that it is true in the main; other
evidence confirms the statement that Lysippus established a type that was regarded as normal by later
art. He is also recorded, probably on the same
authority, to have made great improvements in the
rendering of the hair, and to have shown remarkable
originality in his treatment of symmetry, and in the
variety he introduced into the square build used by
earlier sculptors. The saying is attributed to him that
"while others had made men as they were, he had
made them as they appeared to the eye."[1] He also
carried delicacy of execution into every detail of his
work. A good deal of this criticism, like that of his

---

[1] The Latin is *quales viderentur esse*. The meaning seems quite
clear, though it has been disputed.

study of proportion, applies not so much to Lysippus himself as to the whole art of the fourth century. Yet it is appropriate in its context; for, to later artists, Lysippus represented the sum of the attainments of Greek sculpture as developed in the fourth century; it was through him that these attainments were transmitted to Hellenistic art, and in his work that they were probably seen in their completest form.

Perhaps the most remarkable of all these statements about Lysippus is the assertion, put into his own mouth, that he made men not as they actually were, but as they appeared to the eye. Here we seem to recognise the essential principle of impressionism in art; and, as a matter of fact, we do find some traces of an impressionist treatment in the surviving sculpture of the fourth century—notably in the works of Scopas, and also to some extent in the *Hermes* of Praxiteles, especially in the treatment of the hair. It is to be observed that this tendency is only found in originals of the fourth century; in copies made from them it almost always disappears with the other subtler qualities of expression. We must, however, remember that throughout this criticism of Lysippus there is an implied comparison with Polyclitus; the close, wire-like surface of the hair of the *Doryphorus* is evidently an attempt to render the actual form and texture of the natural object; and so offers a strong contrast to the freer, more pictorial treatment common even in bronze work of the fourth century. Whether the criticism applies to Lysippus in particular, more than to his contemporaries, it is difficult for us to judge, for valuable as the new statue from Delphi is to us, it is a marble work, and probably not from the master's own hand.

About the life of Lysippus we know very little. He is said to have begun as a workman in a bronze-foundry, and to have had no artistic training in his youth; he was encouraged to venture on sculpture by a saying of the painter Eupompus that no master was necessary; he pointed to a crowd of men—perhaps athletes exercising on the palæstra—and said, "Imitate nature, not another artist." This tale seems at first sight inconsistent with the current notion of Lysippus as an academic sculptor. But the innovations which he introduced into the athletic type were the result of his own original observation; it was not his fault if his successors reproduced them in a mechanical and unintelligent manner.

He was an extraordinarily prolific sculptor, if we may credit the tale that he placed a gold coin from every commission he received in a special receptacle, and that, when his heirs broke this open, it was found to contain 1500 coins. Such a number also implies an exceptionally long career. In scale, his works varied

from a colossal figure forty cubits high to a statuette
fit to place on a dining-table, though in this it is
specially noted that the minute scale was not in-
compatible with grandeur of conception.

His works were widely distributed over the mainland
of Greece and Magna Græcia, but no works of his, with
the exception of one at Lampsacus, are recorded as
existing in Asia Minor, where so much of the best
work of Scopas and Praxiteles was to be seen.   This
is the more remarkable, as the eastern schools of Greek
sculpture were to a great extent founded by his pupils.
Though his artistic connection with Alexander was of
the greatest influence both on his career and on the
whole subsequent history of Greek sculpture, he probably did not live long enough to share in the spread
of Greek culture and art to the East in the wake of
Alexander's conquests.   The latest work of his that
can be dated is in connection with the founding of
Cassandrea in 316 B.C. ; for his portrait of *Seleucus*
may well have been made before 312 B.C., when
Seleucus assumed the title of king.   On the other
hand, his statue of the athlete *Troilus,* who won for
the second time in 368 B.C., would make him a contemporary of Praxiteles and Scopas.   He must, however, have survived them both by many years, and his
most famous works seem to fall into the later half of

the fourth century; perhaps the half-century from 366–316 B.C. may be taken as probably covering the period of his artistic activity.

When we turn from literary evidence to the extant statues that can be associated with the name of Lysippus, the first place must be assigned to the statue of the pancratist *Agias*, found by the French excavators at Delphi. This statue was one of a series dedicated by a Thessalian named Daochus; and in Thessaly there existed a duplicate set, with the identical inscription, and the addition, in the case of *Agias*, of the name of Lysippus as sculptor. The original by Lysippus, presumably in bronze, was doubtless set up in Thessaly; but the statues in Delphi must have been contemporary replicas in marble. They are of interest to the history of art as being the first well-attested examples known to us of such replicas, though it is likely enough that, when statues of famous athletes were set up in their own native town as well as in the great Panhellenic shrine where their victories had been gained, the two were often replicas by the same hand. But, for our immediate purpose, the chief importance of the statue of *Agias* lies in the fact that it must bear a very close relation to the work of Lysippus himself. It is not indeed likely to be from his own hand; it has not the finish we should expect in a masterpiece, and its being in marble has probably modified to some extent the character of the bronze original. But, as a contemporary replica, made, in all probability, in the master's own studio, it has a claim on our attention beyond any later copy; and the freshness, vigour and individuality of the work are fully in accordance with our expectations. The general proportions of the body are such as we should look for in a Lysippean work[1]—the small head and the lithe and active but somewhat slender proportions of body and limbs—and the well-balanced poise of the figure increases this appearance of lightness. The sketchy but masterly modelling contrasts strongly with the rather laboured anatomy of the *Apoxyomenos*, and serves at once to relegate the latter to the more academic surroundings of the Hellenistic age.

But it is above all in the treatment and expression of the face that the *Agias* gives us a new conception of the art of Lysippus. The eyes have the same depth of socket and consequent intensity of expression that we have noticed in heads by Scopas; there is, indeed, a considerable resemblance in the *Agias* to a whole series of works that have, since the discovery of the Tegea heads, been generally considered as made under

1 The lower part of both legs, about the ankle, is a clumsy restoration, and a little too short;

PLATE LXVII

**HEAD OF AGIAS. AFTER** *FOUILLES DE DELPHES,* IV., LXIV

*To face p.* 218

the influence of Scopas, if not copied from his works.
There is, however, a contrast as well as a resemblance;
the effect is similar, but the means by which it is produced are different. In the Scopas heads we observed
the heavy mass of flesh above the outer corner of
each eye, which was consistent with the breadth of
the brow and the massive build of the head. In
the *Agias*, which is of slighter proportions, there is
no such over-shadowing of the outer corners of the
eye; but the inner corners of the eye are set very
deep in the head and very close together; the inner
corners of the eye-sockets form acute angles, running
up close to one another and leaving between them only
a narrow ridge for the base of the nose; thus they offer
a strong contrast to the line of the brow, arching away
in a broad curve from the solid base of the nose and
forming an obtuse angle with it, such as we see in
the Scopaic heads. The resultant expression, also, is
different, though in both alike it has a vigour and
intensity such as, until a few years ago, was unknown in
the extant remains of Greek art. In the *Agias* we see,
not the far-away look that is characteristic of the
Scopaic heads, but a more concentrated expression;
the gaze of the eyes is fixed upon some object not very
far away, with a keenness that almost forces the
spectator to look in the same direction. Technically

this may be noted as a deviation from the true principles of sculpture, in a statue, though not in a group; it certainly is an anticipation of the dramatic tendencies of the Hellenistic age.

As regards the proportions of body and limbs, we have already noticed that in their slimness, as compared with the Polyclitan *Doryphorus*, they are characteristic of the traditional reputation of Lysippus. The somewhat sketchy character of the work seems to imply that we have to do with a freely carved replica rather than with a laboured copy of the bronze original, but even after allowing for this, we may still see differences of proportion and muscular development between the *Agias* and the *Apoxyomenos* which are essential, not accidental. The contrast has been well summarised in the following description by Mr. K. T. Frost:[1] "In the *Apoxyomenos* the whole conception of the human figure, the whole athletic ideal, is different. The *Apoxyomenos* has the tendencies of *Agias* toward length of limb and lightness of frame carried a step further. The *Agias* is alert, but it is the alertness of stability; the *Apoxyomenos*, lightly poised, seems able to spring off in either direction : the waist tapers more, the limbs are yet longer, and are made to seem even longer in proportion to the body

1 J. H. S., xxiii. p. 130 note (quoted by Prof. P. Gardner).

PLATE LXVIII

"APOXYOMENOS," IN VATICAN

*To face p. 220*

than they really are.   Compare, for example, the lower
legs of the two "—(allowing, of course, for the fact that
the thick and rather clumsy ankles of the *Agias* are a
restoration)—" in the *Apoxyomenos* the muscles of the
calf are short and swelling, while the tendons which
taper from calf to ankle contribute to the grace which
permeates the entire design.   In the *Agias*, and in the
elder *Sisyphus*, the calf muscles are longer and the
lower portions of the legs fuller.   The hollow back of
the *Apoxyomenos*, the way in which the muscles sweep
inward at the waist from above, and outwards below,
while the steel-like subsidiary tendons and sinews
prevent the slimness from suggesting any lack of
strength, find no counterpart in the *Agias*, whose back
is treated rather sketchily, and whose waist, though
fine, depends more for its strength on the general
solidity of the frame than on specially developed
muscles.   It is difficult to believe that the two statues
represent works by the same artist : it is not only the
type of man, but the way in which that type is expressed that forms the contrast.   The *Apoxyomenos*,
however, compares well with the *Fighting Warrior of
Agasias :* both have the physical character which we
associate with the thoroughbred, and towards which
Greek art seems to have progressed."

If, then, we admit this essential difference, not only

of physical type, but also of artistic execution, between
the *Agias* and the *Apoxyomenos*, any further attempt
to appreciate and to criticise the work of Lysippus
must depend on the manner in which we explain this
difference. Either we must accept both works as
characteristic of the master, and devise some explanation
for the great variation in his style, or else we must
regard one of the two as characteristic and reject the
other as only showing traces of his influence. The
latter course is, perhaps, the safer and more logical;
and, if one of the two must go, there is no doubt that
the connection of the *Agias* with Lysippus rests on the
stronger evidence. If so, we may see in the *Apoxyomenos* one of a well-known series of works, including the
*Praying Boy* at Berlin, and others which we must
notice in the next chapter; and in this series we recognise the systematic and academic development of the
canons of art laid down by Lysippus; it may even be
admissible to recognise in it a recorded work by one of
his pupils, the *Perixyomenos* of Daippus.[1] Those, however, who hesitate to give up an identification that is so
familiar and has met with so universal an acceptance,
must appeal to the length of the artistic career of
Lysippus; they must suggest that when he was young
he fell under the influence of Scopas, though he must

1 As suggested by Prof. P. Gardner, *art. cit.*

at an early stage have adopted the lighter proportions which are characteristic of his work, and have attained the vigour and intensity of expression by a different method. Then, if the *Apoxyomenos* is also to be assigned to him, he must in the latter part of his career have cultivated, in association with his pupils, a more studied and anatomical rendering of the body, and have preferred a different athletic type. At the same time he must have substituted for the keenly individual glance we see in the *Agias* a more generalised and meaningless expression. This expression may, of course, have been still further toned down by the copyist, as we have seen in the case of the *Meleager*. It is possible to imagine such an artistic development, from the fresh vigour and impressionable nature of youth to the academic and laboured style of mature age. But the assumption is hardly justified by the evidence; and it seems better, at least in judging as to the attribution of other statues to Lysippus, to refer them to the standard of the *Agias* rather than, as hitherto, to that of the *Apoxyomenos*.

No works of Lysippus were more famous in ancient times than his portraits of Alexander; and there has been much speculation among modern writers as to which of the many portraits of Alexander that we possess should be assigned to a Lysippean origin. At

first sight the problem seems a simple one, for Plutarch
says that to Lysippus alone was given the privilege of
making portraits of Alexander.   But this cannot mean
more than that Lysippus was appointed portrait sculptor to the Macedonian Court; for Plutarch states that
Lysippus was so selected because Alexander preferred
his portrait to those made by others.  We have records,
also, of other portraits, notably that by Leochares in
the Philippeum at Olympia; and the great demand for
idealised portraits of the conqueror to set up in
the many cities he or his successors had founded must
have led to a corresponding supply.  The portrait by
Lysippus was, however, the finest of all, and was preferred by Alexander himself because Lysippus alone
"displayed his character and showed his manliness as
well as his beauty of feature, while others, striving to
imitate the turn of his neck and the liquid and melting
glance of his eyes, lost his virile and leonine aspect."
There are many epigrams about the portrait; perhaps
the most instructive is the following:

The bronze, methinks, will speak with eyes upraised to Zeus on high,
"I set the earth beneath my feet ; 'tis thine to rule the sky."

Most of the attempts hitherto made to select among
the portraits of Alexander the type which is to be
assigned especially to Lysippus have started from the
assumption that the *Apoxyomenos* must be taken as

PLATE XLIX

HEAD OF ALEXANDER, IN BRITISH MUSEUM

*To face p.* 225

typical of his style ; and, as a not unnatural result, the
Azara head in the Louvre, an idealised portrait of comparatively cold and correct workmanship, has often
been taken as nearest to the Lysippean original. One
might well hesitate about this inference, for in this
head one certainly misses the fire which one of the
epigrams attributes to the work of Lysippus. But now
that we have the *Agias* for comparison, the Azara head
is out of the question, except as showing some faint
reflection of the Lysippean school.

On the other hand, the splendid head from Alexandria
in the British Museum, here reproduced, now for the
first time appears in its proper light. So long as it was
thought that intense individuality and vivid portrayal
of character were alien to the calm dignity of Greek art
in the fourth century, there was a tendency to assign
this head to the Hellenistic age. But the Tegea heads
have enlightened us as to vigour of expression in the
fourth century, and the Agias has shown us that this
vigour must be assigned to Lysippus as well as to
Scopas. The modelling of the British Museum head
shows a directness and simplicity that contrasts with the
laboured and often exaggerated mannerism with which
strong dramatic effect is often associated in Hellenistic
art, notably that of the Pergamene sculptors ; to realise
this, one has only to compare the smooth brow and

P

even sweep of the muscles in this *Alexander* and the knotty and restless treatment which we see in such a head as that represented on Pl. LXXXI. The hair, too, and general contour of the face, reminds us of the *Eubuleus,* so much so that one is sometimes tempted to call the *Eubuleus* " Alexandroid " in type ; yet no one disputes that it belongs to the fourth century. When we examine the *Alexander* more in detail, we find in it a curious combination of characteristics that we have already noticed in other works attributed to masters of fourth-century sculpture. The eyes set in deep at their inner corners remind us of the *Agias ;* but they are also overshadowed at their outer corners by the heavy roll of flesh, curving beneath the brow, which we noticed in the Tegean heads of Scopas. This form of brow may, however, have been a personal peculiarity of Alexander, for we see it strongly indicated in his portrait on coins.[1] With the upturned gaze and the delicate rendering of the lower eyelid, it gives just that impression of power combined with passionate sensibility which is recorded as peculiar to the portrait by Lysippus. The mouth is full, with a hint of sensuality and even of cruelty ; but the whole expression of the face is that of a generous if unbridled nature ; though his weaknesses are not altogether concealed—as in the

[1] *See* P. Gardner, " Types of Greek Coins," xii. 16.

PLATE LXX

ALEXANDER IN COMBAT, FROM SIDON SARCOPHAGUS.  DETAIL FROM HAMDY-BEY AND REINACH,
*NÉCROPOLE ROYALE À SIDON*, PL. XXX

slight twist of the neck—yet the virile and leonine
aspect is that of the great champion of Hellenism, who
could not merely win battles but could spread throughout the civilised world the ideas to which he himself
was passionately devoted. Beside this portrait all the
others sink into insignificance, and in our new knowledge
of the style of Lysippus, we need not hesitate to ascribe to
him the original of a head which justifies the preference given by Alexander himself to his chosen sculptor.
In addition to individual portraits of Alexander,
Lysippus also made some groups in which the Macedonian king was represented in battle or in the chase,
surrounded by his chosen companions. One of these
was a group of bronze equestrian portraits, set up in
Macedonia in memory of those who fell at the battle of
the Granicus; another was a group of bronze figures
dedicated at Delphi, representing Alexander in combat
with a lion, and Craterus coming to his aid. These
groups are lost; but we are enabled to form some
notion of what they were like from the reliefs that
ornament the marble sarcophagus of a king of Sidon
who was evidently an associate of Alexander. On two
sides of this sarcophagus we see combats between Mace-
donians and Persians on horseback and on foot; and
several of these figures are evidently portraits, including
one of Alexander himself. On the other two sides are

hunting scenes, in which Greeks and Orientals are engaged together. The chief group represents a horseman in Persian dress attacked by a lion, while a Greek, probably again Alexander, gallops up to his aid. The resemblance in subject between these reliefs and the bronze groups attributed to Lysippus is most striking, and seems to justify us in supposing that the sarcophagus is the work of a pupil of Lysippus or of a sculptor working under his influence; the probability of such an assumption is increased by the fact that similar scenes of hunting and battle are recorded as made by Euthycrates, the son of Lysippus. The spirited group of Alexander striking at a warrior in Persian dress, whose horse has been wounded or borne down by the charge, is here reproduced as an example of the combat scenes. From this one can realise how the crowded composition and the varied action of the figures suggests the *mêlée* of battle, even though it breaks up into the usual series of pairs of combatants. We find a marked contrast to the slabs of the Mausoleum frieze, where every figure stands out clearly defined against its own bit of background, and the action, however violent, is almost all in one plane. Here there is a suggestion of depth, and the figures sometimes seem to recede into the background or to advance out of it. It is, however, above all the expression and character in

PLATE LXXI

HEAD OF ALEXANDER; DETAIL FROM HAMDY-BEY AND REINACH,
*OP. CIT.*, PL. XXXIII

*Between pp.* 228 *and* 229

PLATE LXXII

HEAD OF PERSIAN; DETAIL FROM HAMDY-BEY AND REINACH,
*OP. CIT.* PL. XXXII

*To face p.* 229

the faces that is remarkable, and it is greatly increased by the fortunate circumstance that the original colouring is, in many cases, well preserved. We see the effect of this addition of colour in the head of a *Persian*, which, as well as the head of *Alexander* himself, is reproduced here on a larger scale. The contrast between the two is notable—on the one hand, the impetuous Macedonian, with his solid and powerful build and irresistible force of intellect; on the other, the sensitive and delicately made Oriental, with his refined features and expressively dark eyes. There is even a beginning of cosmopolitan feeling in the sympathetic rendering of the contrasted national types, even though the theme be the triumph of Hellene over barbarian. The intensity of the expression in each case is yet another example to refute the current notion that Greek art cannot express character and individuality. These reliefs cannot, of course, be associated directly with Lysippus; but they supplement our knowledge of his work and of that of his pupils and associates, and show us how, even in groups of combatants such as he made for Alexander, the expression of passion was no more alien to the art of Lysippus than to that of Scopas.

Returning now to statues recorded as the work of Lysippus himself, we find among them many statues of gods and heroes, varying in size from a colossus

sixty feet high to a statuette of exquisite workmanship
suitable for a table ornament. He made many statues
of gods, and in some of them he probably fixed the type
that became prevalent in the Hellenistic age. The
colossus just mentioned was a statue of *Zeus* set up at
Tarentum—an anticipation in its scale of the more
famous colossus of the *Sun-god* at Rhodes, made by
Chares, the pupil of Lysippus; and at Rhodes there
was also a chariot group by Lysippus himself, representing the *Sun*. At Tarentum there was another
colossal figure, transferred later to Rome, and thence to
Constantinople, a representation of Heracles seated
upon a rock, and leaning his head on his hand, as if
brooding over his labours. This conception of the
weary Heracles as the man of sorrows is not altogether
new; we could even see some anticipation of it in the
Myronic *Heracles*. But it is now emphasised in a
manner characteristic of a more reflective age, and
may almost be said to dominate later art. We see
another example of it in the well-known Farnese
*Heracles* at Naples, itself a later exaggeration of a
type that probably goes back to Lysippus; there we
see the hero not seated but leaning upon his club; and
the expression of the face, too, is that of the hero who
suffers and is weary. A counterpart to this conception is
to be seen in the *Heracles Epitrapezius*, a bronze statuette

less than a foot high, which is said to have formed part
of the table service of Alexander. In this statuette
Heracles was represented in relaxation, seated upon
a rock with a wine-cup in his hand, as if carousing
himself and inviting others to do the same. This side
also, of the life of Heracles is not new either to literature or art; it is familiar to us in Euripides' *Alcestis*,
where the hero's drunken praises of love and wine form
the foil to his strenuous labours and heroic enterprise. But the expression of this human character and
personality in monumental art shows us once more
Lysippus as able, no less than Scopas and Praxiteles, to
express individuality and mood by his art. If we saw
in Myron the beginnings of the study of the psychology
as well as of the physical type of the athlete, we may
surely see the culmination of that study in Lysippus;
and in the ideal athlete, Heracles, it finds its fullest
expression.

Lucian, in his *Zeus Tragœdus*, has occasion to
mention the most representative statues of various
deities, and quotes both the *Posidon* and the *Dionysus*
of Lysippus, as well as his *Heracles*. Unfortunately,
we have no certain criteria for selecting the Lysippean
type from the numerous extant statues of these two
gods. But in the case of the sea-god at least we find a
type of face common in Hellenistic times, and very

probably going back to a Lysippean origin.   In earlier
times *Posidon* is scarcely differentiated from *Zeus*,
except by his attributes ; but in these later heads we
see the indications of the wild and restless nature of
the sea, and even in some instances the weather-beaten
features that suit an old sea-captain rather than a god.
Lysippus very likely did not go so far as this ; but in
this case also it is likely that he originated the individuality of the type.   It has been suggested that we
may with some probability recognise in the *Lateran
Posidon*, which represents the god standing with his
right foot raised on the prow of a ship and his right
elbow resting on his knee, a copy of the statue by
Lysippus.   This position, with its half-turn of the
figure, is suitable both to the artistic tendencies of the
time and to the impatient and fretful nature of the
elemental god.   If not to be attributed to Lysippus, it
certainly shows his influence, and is just such a statue
as he might have produced.   The motive of the raised
foot is not uncommon in later Greek art, and its
prevalence is often attributed to Lysippean influence,
though the position is not unknown in earlier sculpture
—for example, in the Parthenon frieze.   It appears
also in a statue of *Alexander* at Munich, which is
therefore, by some authorities, attributed to Lysippus.
We may see a later variation of it, of the Lysippean

school, in the statue of *Hermes* binding on his sandal (sometimes called *Jason*), in the Louvre.

Another side of the versatile invention of Lysippus is seen in an allegorical figure which has been of great influence on all later art and imagery, his statue of *Opportunity*. Bacon quotes "the common verse": "Occasion turneth a bald noddle after she hath presented her locks in front, and no hold taken"; and this and other similar conceits are derived from the statue by Lysippus; but in Greek καιρός, being masculine, is personified as a boy. He glides forward with winged feet on tip-toe, and holds in one hand a razor, on the edge of which, most probably, was balanced the beam of the scales that typified the sway of fortune. So much we learn from various epigrams that describe the statue, and from a relief that is a more or less free copy of it. We evidently have here an allegory of an elaborate type, similar to that we find in the picture of *Calumny* by the contemporary painter Apelles. To us it seems rather forced and frigid, but it certainly hit the taste of the time; for it led to many imitations, and persisted in Roman and Renaissance art.

In speaking of Scopas, we have already noticed a series of statues—notably the *Meleager* and the Lansdowne *Heracles*—which have considerable resemblance to the *Agias*. Some even go so far as to infer that one or both of these statues must be assigned to Lysippus rather than to Scopas. Our discussion of Scopas has not favoured this view; but the possibility of such a suggestion shows how much the influence of Scopas has affected Lysippus, and how much the two sculptors have in common. Both had a great influence on the art of the Hellenistic age, above all Lysippus through his sons and pupils. He seems, indeed, to have anticipated in his work many of the tendencies of later art, though we have to look to the centuries that followed him for their full development.

# CHAPTER IX

## HELLENISTIC SCULPTURE

AFTER the great sculptors of the fourth century and their immediate pupils, Pliny states that there followed a period of stagnation in art. And although modern critics are disposed to attribute this statement to the fact that the authorities on whom he depended happened to fail him at this point, it is still true that we know the names of no sculptors of this time who can be placed in the same category as the masters with whom we have so far been concerned. There were, doubtless, sculptors after Lysippus, just as there were sculptors before Myron ; but in a book which professes to deal with six representative Greek sculptors, it seems, perhaps, superfluous to say anything about the art of the Hellenistic age. As, however, we found it necessary to take a brief survey of pre-Myronic sculpture, in order to understand what were the achievements of the masters of the fifth century, so it is instructive to notice a few at least of the more characteristic productions of

235

post-Lysippean artists, because in them we see reflected, and sometimes exaggerated, the influence of the masters of the fourth century. And this is the more desirable, because in many cases we only have copies or imitations of the works of these masters themselves, and these copies were made in the Hellenistic age, or later for the Roman market. It is necessary, therefore, in any attempt to appreciate the art of the fifth and fourth century in Greece, to make allowance for such tendencies or characteristics in extant statues as belong to the time when they were actually made rather than to the time to which we must assign the originals from which they are derived.

In the earlier part of the Hellenistic age we find the influence of three great sculptors, Praxiteles, Scopas and Lysippus, still paramount, sometimes separate, sometimes in varying combinations. The isolation of the various schools seems to have been to a great extent broken down; and as, after the conquests of Alexander, first a Panhellenic and then even a cosmopolitan spirit prevailed, so in sculpture also it would depend more upon the individual predilections of the artist than on his local origin to which of the earlier masters he looked chiefly for inspiration; much might also depend on the subject with which he was dealing. If grace and beauty of form were his chief aim. he would follow the lead of

Praxiteles; if passion and dramatic force, that of Scopas; while those who sought either to carry still further the special study of athletic types, or to commemorate historical events by monumental sculptures, probably looked mainly to Lysippus as their master; it is probable, for example, that the sculptors of the great Pergamene school are to be ranked among his followers, though they doubtless owe much to Scopas.

Owing to the scarcity of statues that can be assigned with certainty to the great sculptors, it has already been necessary to quote, in illustration of their style, various works which can only be assigned to their pupils or their influence. Some of these may belong chronologically to a later period; and on the other hand, some of the examples referred to in the present chapter perhaps belong to the fourth century; in some cases there is even a dispute whether they should not be assigned to one or other of the masters whom we have discussed. It is hard to draw a definite line: the present chapter must, therefore, in some degree be regarded as an appendix to the three that immediately precede it.

An instance that lies upon this border-line is offered by the well-known group of the *Niobids*. Pliny tells us that in his time it was a matter of dispute whether this group was made by Scopas or Praxiteles; and many

modern writers on sculpture have assigned them to the
one or the other, according to their own opinion.   But
it is now more generally held that such a statement as
Pliny's carries little weight, and that a work which was
open to such dispute could hardly be by either.   Before
considering these *Niobids*, it will be better to look at
another statue that has sometimes been associated with
them, the *Kneeling Youth* found at Subiaco.   There is
hardly any figure surviving from ancient times about
which artists are more enthusiastic; and their admiration is justified by the extraordinary beauty of the
figure, the softness and sensitiveness of the modelling,
the elasticity and warmth of the flesh; it would be hard
to quote a better example of the marble that seems to
live.   All these are Praxitelean qualities, and it is no
wonder that a suggestion has been made to identify the
statue as an original by Praxiteles himself.   It is
perhaps, however, more probable that we should see in
it a work of the Praxitelean school; the elastic appearance of living flesh is especially noted in a group by the
sons of the master.   The motive of the statue has given
rise to endless discussion, and there seems no chance of
any final explanation; all that can be said is that the
whole character of the figure precludes the notion of
any athletic subject.   The position may be difficult to
explain now that the statue is mutilated; but it is

PLATE LXXIII

STATUE OF A YOUTH, FROM SUBIACO

To face p. 238

clearly chosen in order to display to the utmost the beauty of the modelling; and this seems to be the intention of the artist rather than the simple and direct rendering of any definite action. It is also to be noted that the figure is not worked from any two or three chief aspects, as is usual with Greek statues of the fifth or even the fourth century, but displays new beauties from almost any point of view; it is, in fact, thought out as well as worked completely in the round. In this, as well as in the choice of pose, we see characteristics that belong to the early Hellenistic age or perhaps the close of the fourth century rather than to an earlier date. We may then probably recognise in the youth from Subiaco the most perfect extant example of the Praxitelean tradition—a tradition which survives into Græco-Roman art, though in later works the desire for grace and softness of modelling is rarely if ever coupled with the distinction of form and direct observation of nature which contribute to the charm of this figure.

The question of the *Niobids* is a very large one, which can only be touched on here in its main outlines. The subject of the punishment of Niobe and her children for her overweening boast is a common one in the art of all periods. The form it usually takes is a representation of her children, both sons and daughters, transfixed by the arrows of Apollo and

Artemis, while she herself appeals for mercy or vainly
strives to shield them.   The set of statues now in
Florence is generally associated with the statement
of Pliny as to the authorship of Scopas or Praxiteles,
though it is generally admitted that they are only
copies, not the originals brought by Sosius to Rome
from Cilicia.   They were mostly found near the
Lateran at Rome;   more than one example exists of
some of the figures, notably the fine Chiaramonti
statue in the Vatican, which represents one of the
daughters advancing rapidly;   her rich, flowing drapery
is treated in a more impressive, but less simple, style
than we see in most of the figures at Florence;
it shows, indeed, something of the restless and tempestuous character we often find in Hellenistic work.
It is, however, more vigorous and spirited than the
corresponding statue at Florence ; yet those who maintained a fourth-century origin for the group were
constrained to regard it as less faithful to its original
than the tamer copies.   The discussion has, however,
been much widened in scope by the discovery, or
identification, due to Professor Furtwängler, of a set of
statues of *Niobids* which belong to about the middle
of the fifth century ; and these not only deal with the
same subject, but repeat some of the identical groups
and figures which we see in the later set, though the

PLATE LXXIV

DISC WITH DEATH OF NIOBIDS, IN BRITISH MUSEUM

*To face p.* 241

style and execution are totally different.  This need
not surprise us, when we remember that the subject of
the slaying of the Niobids occurs on fifth-century vases,
that it was represented by Phidias on the throne of
the Olympian *Zeus*, and that it is frequently repeated
upon later reliefs ; for example, upon the marble disc
now in the British Museum, and here reproduced.
Upon these various works we find the same figures—
that is to say, figures in the same position and action
—recurring again and again.  It seems that each artist
selected from a répertoire of figures appropriate to
the scene those that best suited his composition, and
carried them out in detail according to his own style
and technique.  Whether Scopas or Praxiteles contributed anything directly to the treatment of the
group it is hard to say.  But the extant figures seem
mostly to belong to a set that were mounted upon a
rocky basis, suggesting the heights of Mount Sipylos,
where the tragedy occurred.  Of the various groups
that made up the composition, none is more familiar
than that of the mother clasping her youngest daughter
close to her knees, and holding a fold of drapery over
her head, as if in a vain effort to shelter her from the
destroying arrows ; in the agonised expression of her
face the influence of Scopas is certainly to be traced.
This group probably appeared in the centre of the

marble disc, though only the foot of Niobe and the upper curve of her drapery can now be seen. Another group, which we can see to the left upon the disc, represents a brother holding up his chlamys to shelter one of his sisters,[1] who is already wounded and has sunk down, leaning back against his knee. The separate figure of the brother, without that of the sister, here reproduced from the statue in Florence, shows the character of this series. We can see in it a softness and elasticity of modelling, and a graceful realism in the treatment of drapery that reminds us of Praxiteles; and an intensity of expression, enhanced by the shadow thrown on the eye by the brow and on the brow by the overhanging mass of drapery, that resembles what we see in the work of Scopas. It is interesting to note how this motive of the overshadowing drapery has been translated by the sculptor of the disc into a comparatively commonplace treatment of the rich folds of drapery as a background and frame to the figures. But these resemblances to the work of Scopas and Praxiteles do not imply that either of these masters made a group of the *Niobids* from which the extant figures are directly copied. They must rather be

[1] The position of the right and left arms is inverted on the disc probably to make the representation in relief easier and more effective.

PLATE LXXV

A SON OF NIOBE, IN FLORENCE

To face p. 242

PLATE LXXVI

HEAD, IN BRITISH MUSEUM

*To face p.* 243

regarded as a characteristic product of the early Hellenistic age, with its tendency to imitate the work of the great masters of the fourth century, and often to combine together the qualities of different schools.

Another head that has sometimes been connected with the *Niobids* is that of a youthful hero in the British Museum; it was once part of a statue, and is looking up with an anxious expression. Stark actually identified it as one of the sons of Niobe; but the type of head is rather that which is generally assigned to the school of Lysippus, resembling the *Apoxyomenos* rather than the *Agias;* though it has something of the vigour of expression of the latter, this is probably to be interpreted in relation to the probable action of the statue; unless, indeed, it be rightly identified as belonging to the Lysippean type of Hermes, binding his sandals while he looks up for orders to Zeus. There is, in any case, a certain dramatic quality in this head, as in the *Niobids* also, which anticipates the more sensational work that we find later among the Pergamene sculptures. The seated bronze *Hermes* of Naples is another statue of about the same period and tendencies, and is generally recognised as belonging to the school of Lysippus. The light and agile pose of the figure, seated on a rock from which at any moment he seems ready to start

upon his mission, reminds us of the agile poise of the
*Apoxyomenos*.  The same may be said of the slight and
graceful proportions of the figure and of the type of
head; but here, since we have a bronze original, not a
marble copy, we can judge better of the effect intended
by the artist.  The face, however, though pleasing, has
less character, and shows a tendency towards that
generalised academic style which often prevails in
Hellenistic work, and has gone far to create the
modern notion of the lack of individuality in ancient
sculpture.  Thus the quality that is, perhaps, the most
essential in genuine Greek work of the fourth century
is already fading away, and giving place to the vague
generalisation which we see in much Græco-Roman
work.

Another example showing this same tendency in an
even more marked degree is also among the few life
size bronze statues that have survived from ancient
times.  This is the statue from Cerigotto now in
Athens.  The chance discovery of this statue, together
with the rest of a wrecked cargo of sculptures which
was evidently among the plunder of Greece on its way
to Rome, is among the most interesting romances of
modern days.  Whether the cargo was due to military
or commercial enterprise, it is evidently miscellaneous,
and gives no clue as to the nature of any statue forming

PLATE LXXVII

HEAD OF BRONZE HERMES AT NAPLES

*To face* **p.** 244

PLATE LXXVIII

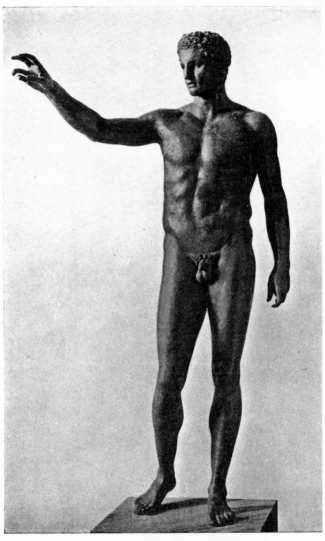

BRONZE STATUE, FROM WRECK OFF CERIGOTTO, IN ATHENS

*To face p.* 245

part of it, except that all must have been carried off from Greece before the time of the wreck, which is dated by the contents of the ship about the beginning of the first century B.C. Some writers have tried to identify this bronze as a work of the fourth or even the fifth century, an attempt that cannot bear the test of a careful analysis of the style of the statue. It represents an athlete standing with his right arm extended, and holding some round object that has now disappeared, his pose recalling to some extent that of the *Apoxyomenos*; the exact meaning of his action appears to be an insoluble problem, but the position is evidently chosen to show off the figure. The head has a good deal of resemblance both to that of the *Hermes* of Praxiteles and to that of the Lansdowne *Heracles*, which, as we have seen, is probably to be connected with Scopas. The modelling of the body, on the other hand, is heavy and laboured, as elaborate as in the *Apoxyomenos*, but without its highly strung muscles. It is, in fact, essentially an eclectic work, combining the characteristics of several of the fourth-century schools, yet falling short of all of them by a lack of distinction in work and an academic quality that again betrays the Hellenistic age. It is a most valuable acquisition to us as a bronze of undoubtedly Greek workmanship, and as preserving much of the beauty of form and skill in execution of which the tradition was still preserved ; but these qualities need not lead us to place it among the original works of the masters whose influence it shows.

Perhaps, however, no statue is so characteristic of the early Hellenistic age as the splendid *Victory* from Samothrace, now mounted on one of the staircases in the Louvre.  This figure was set up in 'the island of Samothrace to commemorate a naval victory ; the goddess was represented as standing on the prow of a ship, holding a trumpet to her lips with one hand, and with the other carrying a trophy over her shoulder. These details, so far as they cannot be seen in the extant portions of the statue, may be learnt from a reproduction of the figure which is found on contemporary coins.  She appears to have just alighted on the ship, and her wings are half folded.  Her rich drapery is swept against and away from her limbs by the rush of the wind, as she leans forward to meet it.  The whole composition is full of imposing vigour and dramatic force ; even in its damaged condition it makes an over- whelming impression, and this must have been even more vivid when the figure was complete, and was set up in the open air amid suitable surroundings.  The half turn of the body above the waist, which gives variety and life to the pose, is a favourite device in Hellenistic art; and the tempestuous lines of the drapery, as it

PLATE LXXIX

VICTORY, FROM SAMOTHRACE, IN THE LOUVRE

*To face p.* 246

is blown across and across the figure, enhances the feeling of exultant haste with which the goddess proclaims her joyful tidings. It is instructive to notice the difference that has come over the spirit of Greek sculpture between the time of this *Victory* and the *Victory* by Pæonius, set up at Olympia some two and a half centuries earlier. There we see the messenger of the gods, floating calmly down from Olympus to carry their award; and the simple and dignified treatment is in accordance with this conception of the subject. The *Victory* of Samothrace, on the other hand, seems to bear the impress of the stress and storm of the combat from which she has come. If the gods became human in the fourth century, in the Hellenistic age, men themselves, following Alexander, were raised to the position of gods, and the victories they won were marked by their own restless genius. It seems peculiarly fitting that this *Victory* should have found her final home in Paris; it has had no small influence on modern French sculpture, which has considerable affinity with it. Modern art has striven in vain to reproduce the calm dignity of the sculpture of the fifth century; nor does the more human grace of the fourth century seem easier to attain without affectation. But this stormy and restless vigour, with which, in the Hellenistic age, the art of Hellas was

spread over the civilised world, seems less unapproach-
able, and finds many parallels among modern works,
though few of them can rival it in originality of
conception and skill of execution.

Among the new centres in which the art of sculpture
flourished under the successors of Alexander, the most
prolific and original was Pergamum, where the kings of
the Attalid dynasty made their capital the rival of
Alexandria in science and literature, and beyond all
rivals in the architecture and sculpture with which it
was enriched.    The sculptors they employed were
attached by tradition to the school of Lysippus, though
more than a century had elapsed since that master's
activity.    We have seen in the *Alexander Sarcophagus* from Sidon an example of the kind of work
that was done for Oriental princes by the pupils of
Lysippus.    At Pergamum we have on a monumental
scale the sculptures made to commemorate the great
victories of Attalus and Eumenes over the Gauls who
had invaded Asia.

It would lead us too far from our subject to discuss
all these sculptures; one figure, that of the well-known
*Dying Gaul* in the Capitoline Museum at Rome, must
suffice to show the relation of the Pergamene sculptures
to what had preceded them.    A wounded warrior is
nothing new in Greek art, nor is the representation of

PLATE LXXX

To face p. 248

DYING GAUL, IN CAPITOLINE MUSEUM, ROME

a barbarian; but as we find them in this statue, they show an immense difference from the work of the fourth century. Curiously enough, this *Dying Gaul* resembles in pose the *Dying Warrior* of the Æginetan pediment, both alike contrasting with such figures, graceful even in death, as we see among the Niobids. Nor is the resemblance altogether accidental; in the Hellenistic work we see a return to the realism which is to be found in much of the finest archaic work, and which had been to some extent submerged during the great period of Hellenic sculpture. In the study both of the physical type and of the character of the Northern barbarian the quality of Pergamene art is most clearly shown; there is abundant knowledge both of anatomy and ethnology, and that not merely superficial, but deep and sympathetic. The Persian warriors on the Sidon *Sarcophagus* showed, indeed, an appreciation of a non-Hellenic type in expression of face as well as in racial characteristics; but the style of the sculpture was the same for Greek and for foreigner. Here, in the uncouth and massive strength of the Gaul, in his hardness of skin and muscle, in his matted hair and wrinkled brow, above all, in the stubborn fortitude with which he meets his death, we find new ideals as well as novelty of subject, that cosmopolitan Hellenism which, while it derives the technique and much of the spirit of its artistic expression from Scopas and from Lysippus, has come to realise the existence of much that is admirable outside the Hellenic pale. The sculptor who made the portrait of *Mausolus* could do justice to a Philhellenic prince without entirely obscuring his foreign traits; but the sculptor who made the *Dying Gaul* has gone beyond this, and embodied with sympathy and insight an altogether un-Hellenic conception. Another head of a *Warrior*, in the British Museum, and probably, though not certainly, of Pergamene work, will also serve to illustrate this side of Hellenistic art. It represents most likely a combatant, again of foreign type, though his nationality is not easy to determine. In the intense expression of the eyes, and the way they are shadowed by the brow, we recognise a treatment derived from Scopas; but in the rough and matted hair, the knotty and exaggerated rendering of sinews and veins, and the restless and mobile brow, there is a contrast to the restraint and moderation which is never absent from fourth-century work, even if it be as vigorous as the Tegea heads or the portrait of *Alexander*. The modern effect produced by such a head as this, in which

> New hopes shine through the flesh they fray,
> New fears aggrandise the rags and tatters,

anticipates in many ways the Christian art of a later date, and suggests at the same time that the reason

PLATE LXXXI

HEAD OF WARRIOR, IN BRITISH MUSEUM

To face p. 250

why such things are not found in Hellenic art is not because earlier sculptors could not, but because they would not produce them. Whether their notions of the limitations of the sculptor's art be right or wrong, it can hardly be disputed that they kept within them, consciously or unconsciously, and that the difference between ancient and modern art is in some degree at least due to these limitations.

It would be easy to pursue further the developments of Hellenistic art, whether in the vigorous and imposing if exaggerated work of the Pergamene and other Asiatic schools, in the somewhat academic style of Greece itself, or in the numerous branches of Græco-Roman art. But the examples already given must suffice to show how, on the one hand, the traditions of the great masters of Greek sculpture persisted through many generations of their successors, how, on the other hand, new and to some extent non-Hellenic influences were at work throughout the Hellenistic world. Some of these influences need detain us the less because they are surprisingly modern in character, and we are here concerned rather to note what is not modern, and therefore is difficult for us to appreciate, among the masterpieces of Hellenic art. It is impossible for us now to see those masterpieces as the Greeks saw them, and as they were meant to be seen. Instead of standing in the luminous and transparent air of Greece, upon sites made beautiful by nature and by art, and hallowed by the most sacred associations, they now have to be studied in the galleries of our museums. Instead of glowing with the life they owed to the painter's brush no less than to the sculptor's chisel, they have emerged from their long burial the colourless abstractions of form that appeal with little force to the eye or to the heart of the uninitiated. Often they are mutilated beyond recognition, or restored by unsympathetic hands, until their original meaning is hard to appreciate ; often they are themselves but later imitations or travesties which contaminate the finer ideals and more distinguished workmanship of the original master with the commonplace conceptions and mechanical technique of a later age. We need imagination as well as knowledge if we would understand and appreciate them. And it should help us in any such attempt if we can realise in any degree the spirit and the character of the great sculptors who are representative of the art of Hellas.

# SELECT BIBLIOGRAPHY

## (a) GENERAL

COLLIGNON, M. "Histoire de la Sculpture Grecque."
Two vols. Paris, 1892–7.

COOK, E. T. "Handbook to the Greek and Roman Antiquities in the British Museum." London, 1903.

FURTWAENGLER, A. "Masterpieces of Greek Sculpture."
Trans. E. SELLERS. London, 1895.

GARDNER, E. A. "Handbook of Greek Sculpture."
Revised Edition. London, 1907.

GARDNER, P. "A Grammar of Greek Art." London, 1905.

LOEWY, E. "The Rendering of Nature in Early Greek Art." Trans. J. FOTHERGILL. London, 1907.

WALTERS, H. B. "The Art of the Greeks." London, 1906.


## (b) SPECIAL

COLLIGNON, M. "Lysippe." Paris, 1905.

"Fouilles de Delphes" (Homolle). Paris.

FURTWAENGLER, A. "Aegina, das Heiligtum der Aphaia." Munich, 1906.

GARDNER, E. A. "Ancient Athens." London and New York, 1902.

HAMDY-BEY and REINACH, TH. "Une Nécropole Royale à Sidon." Paris, 1892.

KLEIN, W. "Praxiteles." Leipsic, 1898.

LECHAT, H. "Phidias." Paris, 1907.

MAHLER, A. "Polyklet und Seine Schule." Athens and Leipsic, 1902.

MURRAY, A. S. "The Sculptures of the Parthenon," London, 1903.

"Olympia—Die Ausgrabungen." Vol. III. "Bildwerke in Stein und Thon (Treu)." Berlin, 1894-7.

PERROT, G. "Praxitèle." Paris, 1904.

WALDSTEIN, C., "Essays on the Art of Pheidias." Cambridge, 1885.

Recent Articles in the following periodicals:
> *Bulletin de Correspondance Hellénique.* Athens.
> Ἐφημερὶς Ἀρχαιολογική. Athens.
> *Jahrbuch des k. deutsch. arch. Instituts.* Berlin.
> *Jahreshefte des k.k. Oesterreich. Instituts.* Vienna.
> *Journal of Hellenic Studies.* London.
> *Mittheilungen des k. deutsch. arch. Instituts in Athen.*
> *Mittheilungen des k. deutsch. arch. Instituts in Rom.*
> *Revue Archéologique.* Paris.

## (c) COLLECTIONS OF ILLUSTRATIONS.

BRUNN, H., and ARNDT. "Denkmäler griechischer und römischer Skulptur." Munich, 1897. Over 600 large plates.

HILL, G. F. "One Hundred Masterpieces of Sculpture." London, 1909.

VON MACH. "Handbook of Greek and Roman Sculpture." Boston, 1905. 500 small plates.

# INDEX

ABERDEEN *Head*, 147, 170
Academic generalisation, 9
Acrolithic technique, 86
Ægina, pedimental groups from, 34–42
Æginetan style, 40
*Agasias, Fighting Warrior of*, 221
Ageladas, teacher of Myron, Phidias and Polyclitus, 58, 60
*Agias*, by Lysippus, 198, 199, 217 *sqq.*
Alcamenes, 151
Alexander, his connection with Lysippus, 216, 223 *sqq.*
    various portraits of, 227
*Amazons*, 131 *sqq.*
    by Phidias, 114
        Polyclitus, 122
        Scopas, 187
Anthropomorphism, Greek tendency to, 16
" Antique, the," 4
Aphæa, sculptures of temple of, 34–42
*Aphrodite* of Cnidus, by Praxiteles, 140, 143
    of Cos, 154
    of Melos, 160
    by Polyclitus, 120
    by Praxiteles, 151–54
    by Scopas, 191
    *Urania*, by Phidias, 114
*Apollo*, Choiseul Gouffier, 115
    *Citharœdus*, 208
    *of the Locusts*, 114
    *and Marsyas*, by Praxiteles, 172

*Apollo*, found near **Mausoleum**, 207
    in Museo delle Terme, 114
    on Olympian pediment, 44
    by Praxiteles, 165
    *Sauroctonus*, 165, 166
    by Scopas, 208
    statues, 118
*Apoxyomenos*, by Lysippus, 210, 211, 218
Archaic smile, 48
Architect of Parthenon, 101
Architectural sculptures, 29
*Ares Ludovisi*, 197
Argive *Hera*, 138
    school, 60, 117, 121, 131, 133, 185, 199, 212
Arles, *Venus* of, 159
Art critics of last century, 8
*Artemis Brauronia*, by Praxiteles, 166, 167, 168
    of Gabii, 166, 167
    by Praxiteles, 165
Artemis, temple of, at Ephesus, 178
Artemisia, wife of Mausolus, 178, 187, 204
Asclepius from Melos, Praxitelean head of, 171
*Asclepius*, by Scopas, 180
Atalanta from Tegea, 184, 186, 189
*Athena* on Acropolis at Athens, by Phidias, 87
    Alea at Tegea, temple of, 178
    *Areia* at Platæa, 85
    birth of, 97

*Athena Parthenos*, by Phidias, 90, 91, 93
  portrait of Phidias on shield of, 82, 83
  at Peilene, by Phidias, 86
*Athenian Heroes* at Delphi, 84
Athenian school, 21, 53, 81
  treasury at Delphi, 33
Athletes, by Lysippus, 212, 215
  by Myron, 58, 59, 175
  heads, by Polyclitus, 129
Attic tombstones, mourning figures on, 173
  showing influence of Scopas, 208

BALANCE of figures in Ægina pediments, 38, 39
Beneventum head, 130
Birth of Athena, 97
Bologna head, 113
*Boy binding on a Fillet*, 128
*Boy crowning himself*, 129
Brunn, 3

CALAMIS, 50, 51, 52, 57
Calydonian boar hunt on temple at Tegea, 180, 181
*Canon* of Polyclitus, 122
  of proportions, 118, 119, 120
Capitoline *Faun*, 163
Carrey's drawings of Parthenon pediments, 97
*Caryatids*, 112
Casts, use of, 4
Cemetery at Athens, sculpture in, 173
*Centaur Metopes* of Parthenon, 95, 97
Centaurs on Olympian pediment, 44
Ceramicus at Athens, 174
Cerigotto, statue from, 244
*Charioteer of Delphi*, 49 *sqq.*
  of Mausoleum, 205

Cimon, 89
Cnidians, Treasury of, 29
Colossal *Hera*, by Polyclitus, 120
  work by Lysippus, 230
  representative of Phidias, 81, 106
Convention in art, 9, 10
Cows from Parthenon frieze, 105
Cresilas, 130
  *Amazon* by, 133, 136
*Cyniscus*, 129

DELPHI, sculpture from, 29-34, 49, 217-223
*Demeter* of Cnidus, 192-195
*Diadumenus* of Polyclitus, 124-128
*Diomed*, 77
Dionysus on Cnidian Treasury, 30
*Dionysus*, by Myron, 71, 72
*Discobolus*, 61-65
  head, 76
Dorian sculpture, 32
*Doryphorus* of Polyclitus, 122-124, 212
Drapery of early statues, 20, 21
  Amazons on Mausoleum, 206
  *Atalanta*, by Scopas, 187
  *Athena Parthenos*, 90
  of *Delphi Charioteer*, 50
  *Demeter* of Cnidus, 194
  gods in different periods, 153, 154, 159, 160
  *Hermes*, by Praxiteles, 148, 149
  *Lemnian Athena*, 112
  *Ludovisi Throne*, 53
  *Mœnad*, by Scopas, 189
  observation of, 23
  Parthenon pediments, 99, 100
  *Victory* from Samothrace, 246

Drawing, influence of, 55
*Dying Gaul*, 248-250

EARLY fifth-century sculpture in Athens, 96
Eclecticism of Hellenistic art, 24, 25
*Eirene and Plutus*, 150
Eleusis, head found near temple of Hades at, 168
Elgin marbles, 6, 28, 29, 79, 80, 82
Ephesus, *Amazons* at, 131-133
   temple of Artemis at, 178
Epidaurus, Tholus at, 179
*Erechtheus*, by Myron, 70
*Eros* of Centocelle, 162
   as infant, 162
   by Praxiteles, 140, 160
*Eubuleus* head from Eleusis, 147, 168, 169, 226
Euphranor, 213
Eupompus, 215
Expression in Greek art, 192, 193, 195


*Farnese, Diadumenus*, 128
   *Hera*, 114, 138
   *Heracles*, 230
*Faun* of Capitol, 163
Free statues, 47
Freehand modelling, 21, 22
Frieze of Cnidian Treasury, 30
   of Mausoleum, 204, 205
   of Parthenon, 101 *et seq.*
Frontality in sculpture, 13, 31, 32, 34, 42
Furtwängler on Æginetan sculpture, 35, 37-40
   on *Lemnian Athena*, 111, 113


GOLD and ivory work by Phidias, 80, 86, 108
   by Polyclitus, 137

Grace, strength sacrificed to, by Hellenistic sculptors, 171
Græco-Roman art, 10
Greeks and Amazons, 82


Hair treatment by Lysippus, 214
   Praxiteles, 156
   Scopas, 191
Harmony of statues, by Polyclitus, 124
Hellenistic age, characteristics of sculpture in, 178
   ideas, 14
*Heifer*, by Myron, 68
*Hera* at Argos, by Polyclitus, 137
   on Argive coins, 137
   *Farnese*, 114, 138
   by Polyclitus, 122
*Heracles*, Aberdeen head, 170
   *Epitrapezius*, 230
   Farnese, 230
   Lansdowne, 198, 199
   by Lysippus at Tarentum, 230
   by Myron, 73
   by Polyclitus, 136
   from Tegea, 184
Heracles and Theseus on Athenian treasury, 33
*Hermes* binding on his sandal, in the Louvre, 233
   *Dionysus*, by Cephisodotus, 151
   by Praxiteles, 142, 143-151, 175
Horse's head from Parthenon pediment, 100, 101
Human aspect of divinity, 160
*Hygieia*, by Scopas, 180


*Iacchus* in British Museum, 115
Ictinus, architect of Parthenon 101
*Idolino* at Florence, 129

" Ilissus," from Parthenon pediment, 98
Illusionism, 14, 15
Individuality in Greek art, 177

LADAS, 59, 68, 69
Lansdowne *Amazon*, 132, 134
    *Heracles*, 198, 199
Lapithæ on Olympian pediment, 44
*Lateran Posidon*, 232
Laurium head, 190, 191
*Lemnian Athena*, 111, 112
Lenormant statuette, 93
Leochares, 203
Lessing, 7, 8
Leto, by Praxiteles, 165, 172
Löwy, 13
*Ludovisi Throne*, 53, 54, 55
Lucian, 24, 231
    on *Lemnian Athena*, 111, 114
    on Praxiteles, 156
*Lycian Sarcophagus*, 115
Lysippus, 203, 210–234
    influence of Scopas on, 198

*Mænad*, by Scopas, 164, 187, 188, 189
Mantinea, statues made by Praxiteles for, 165, 175
Marathon, artistic use of spoils from, 84, 85, 87
*Marsyas*, by Myron, 65, 74
Marsyas and Apollo, by Praxiteles, 172
Mausoleum sculpture, 178, 179, 187, 201–206
Mausolus, tomb of, 178, 187
Medici head, 5
*Meleager*, 5, 6, 28, 195, 196, 198, 223
Memory, working from, 27
*Metopes* of Theseum, 76
    of Parthenon, 75, 95, 96

Miltiades, 85
Model, use of, 9, 21, 25, 26
Mood in Greek art, 177
Mount Helicon, group of *Muses* on, 173
" Mourning women," sarcophagus with, 173
*Muse, Roman Lady as a*, 174
Muses, by Praxiteles, 172, 173
Myron, 56–78, 151

NAUCRATIS, 18
Nelson head, 130
*Nereid* monument, 203
*Niobids*, 237–244
Nude as seen by Greek sculptors, 23
    at Olympia, 46
    treatment of, in Parthenon sculptures, 84
    by Phidias, 98
    by Praxiteles, 148, 153
    of, 155

OBSERVATION in art, 10, 12, 16, 19
Olympia, pediments at, 43
    *Victory* at, 247
Onatas, 47
*Opportunity*, by Lysippus, 233

PÆONIUS, *Victory* by, 247
Palatine *Apollo*, 208
Parian marble, 22, 33
Parium, *Eros* of, 160, 161
Parthenon, 94–106
Passion in Greek art, 177
Pausanias, description of *Athena Parthenos*, by, 91, 92
    at Olympia, 105, 106
    on *Lemnian Athena*, 111
    on temple sculpture, 179, 181
*Peace carrying the Child Wealth*, 150

Pedimental figures from Parthenon, 97, 98, 99
of Mausoleum, 203
from Tegea, 181, &c.
Pellene, 86
Peloponnesian art, characteristics of, 48, 53, 84
Pelops and Œnomaus on Olympian pediment, 44
Pentelic marble, 22
Pergamene sculpture, 248, 249
*Perixyomenos*, 222
*Perseus*, by Myron, 70
*Persephone*, 98
*Persians*, on Sidon sarcophagus, 229
Petworth head, 147, 152, 157, 158
Phidias, 79–116
  *Athena* at Pellene, by, 86
  colossal work of, 81, 87, 90, 93, 106
  friend of Pericles, 89
  gold and ivory work, 80, 93, 108
  portrait of, 82
  treatment of nude by, 98
Phryne, 143, 154, 155, 159, 161, 174
Pliny, 235, 237
  description of *Athena Parthenos*, by, 91
  on Scopas, 200, 201
Politics and art, 42
Polyclitus, 117–139
Portraits by Praxiteles, 159
Pose, development in, 20
*Posidon and Athena*, on Parthenon pediment, 97
  by Lysippus, 231
*Praying Boy* at Berlin, 222
Praxiteles, 140–176
Proportions of body used by Lysippus, 218
Profile conception of sculpture, 13
Pythagoras, of Rhegium, 51, 52

RELIEF, 14
Restoration of Athlete, false, 63
Rhodes, *Sun-god* by Lysippus at, 230
Ruskin on gods in Greek art, 6
  on horses of Parthenon frieze, 103

SAMOTHRACE, *Victory* from, 246
*Satyr*, by Praxiteles, 162, 163, 164, 175, 201
Scopas, 177–209
Sea creatures, by Scopas, 200, 201
Selection in art, 10, 15
*Seleucus*, portrait of, by Lysippus, 216
Self-centred nature of Greek sculpture, 61
Semi-draped *Aphrodites*, date of, 160
Sidon sarcophagus, 115, 173, 203, 227
*Silenus and the Infant Bacchus*, 150
*Sisyphus*, 221
*Sleep*, Praxitelean head of, 171
Spiritual character of Praxiteles' work, 149
Statuette copies of *Athena Parthenos*, 93, 94
Subiaco, youth from, 238, 239
*Sun-god* at Rhodes, by Lysippus, 230

TANAGRA, 171
Tarentum, *Heracles* by Lysippus at, 230
  *Zeus*, by Lysippus at, 230
Tegea, temple of Athena Alea at, 178, 179, 180
Tegean pediments, 181 *sqq.*
Temperament in Greek art, 177
Terra-cotta figurines from Tanagra, 172

Texture rendered by Praxiteles, 149
" Theseus," from Parthenon pediment, 98
Thespiæ, *Eros* of, 160, 161, 162
Thessaly, statues by Lysippus in, 217
Tholos at Epidaurus, 179
*Three Fates*, from Parthenon pediment, 98
Torso of *Atalanta* from Tegea, 187
Townley *Venus*, 159
Transition, Myron, the artist of, 67
Trentham statue, 174
Triton, by Scopas, 200
*Troilus*, portrait of, by Lysippus, 216

Vaison statue, 125
Varvakeion statuette, 93
Vatican *Aphrodite*, 152
    genius of, 162

Vatican *Apollo Citharœdus*, 208
*Venus de' Medici*, 155
Victory on hand of *Athena Parthenos*, 91
*Victory* of Brescia, 160
    from Samothrace, 246
    Pæonius at Olympia, 247
Votive offerings, statues as, 17


Warrior, head of, in British Museum, 250
Westmacott *Athlete*, 129, 132
Winckelmann, 7, 8
*Wounded Amazons*, 130 *sqq.*
    *Philoctetes*, 133


Zeus, at Olympia, by Phidias, 90, 105, 106
    by Lysippus, 230
    *Meilichios*, 122
    *of Otricoli*, 108, 109
    Phidian head of, at Boston, 108, 109